THE SPANISH-AMERICAN WAR

THE SPANISH-
AMERICAN WAR

Edward F. Dolan

The Millbrook Press   Brookfield, Connecticut

Cover photograph courtesy of North Wind Picture Archives

Photographs courtesy of Brown Brothers: pp. 10, 22 (both), 23, 25, 31, 52, 53, 62, 75, 105; Anne S. K. Brown Military Collection, Brown University Library: pp. 18, 65; Culver Pictures, Inc.: pp. 28, 78; U. S. Naval Historical Center: pp. 34, 44; National Archives: p. 55 (#111-SC-89751); North Wind Picture Archives: pp. 81, 87, 90

Published by The Millbrook Press, Inc.
2 Old New Milford Road
Brookfield, CT 06804
www.millbrookpress.com

Library of Congress Cataloging-in-Publication Data
Dolan, Edward F., 1924-
The Spanish-American War / by Edward F. Dolan.
p. cm.
Includes bibliographical references and index.
ISBN 0-7613-1453-9 (lib. bdg.)
1. Spanish-American War, 1898—Juvenile literature.
[1. Spanish-American War, 1898.] I. Title.
E715 .D65   2001
973.8'9—dc21   2001018677

CONTENTS

Chapter 1—A Ship Dies

On the night of February 15, 1898, the American battleship *Maine* lay quietly in the harbor at Havana, Cuba. The time was 9:40. The ship had just seconds left to live.

The *Maine* had steamed into the harbor three weeks before—on January 25—and had dropped anchor several hundred yards offshore. Officially, the warship was making a courtesy call on the Spanish authorities at the Cuban capital. In truth, it was there to take the Americans working in Havana away to safety should their lives be threatened by the current political upheaval in the Spanish-held island.

Cuba, which had been a province of Spain since the late 1400s, was gripped in a revolution, with the island people fighting to be rid of the oppressive rule of their Spanish masters. The struggle had begun in 1895. Just recently, it had caused rioting in Havana, triggering the fear in Washington, D.C., that the American residents there were in danger of being accidentally injured or killed. Further, U.S. businesses were heavily invested in the island and could be harmed by trouble between the Spanish and Cubans. The *Maine* was dispatched on its rescue mission. By the time it arrived, however, quiet had returned to the city.

There was noise in Havana this night of February 15. But there was no anger in the sound. It was made up of the laughter, shouting, and music of Carnival. The people were enjoying the annual celebration just before Lent. The season of fasting and prayer, Lent would begin the next day and continue until Easter. The night itself was overcast, humid, and hot.

The *Maine*, painted white (as were the U.S. warships at the time), glowed softly in the darkness. The

The U.S.S. Maine *at anchor in the harbor in Havana in 1898*

ship was a smallish but impressive warrior, weighing 6,682 tons and capable of a top speed of 16 knots (29,632 meters, or 97,217 feet). It bristled with armament, from four 10-inch (254-millimeter) and six 6-inch (152-millimeter) guns to two 1-pounder (0.5-kilogram) cannons and, below the waterline, four 18-inch (457-millimeter) torpedo tubes. Aboard was a crew of 343 enlisted men and 31 officers. Commanding was Captain Charles D. Sigsbee.

Except for the sailors standing watch, the crewmen had bedded down for the night by 9:30. Two officers were seated on deck at the stern, enjoying their last cigars of the day and looking over at the lights of Havana. Captain Sigsbee was in his cabin, writing a letter to his wife. At 9:40, he began to insert the letter into an envelope. . . .

The Death of a Ship

The *Maine*'s death began with two explosions—a small one that sounded like a gunshot to Sigsbee and a monster one that lifted the ship by the bow, threw it back down, and sent a wrenching shudder all along its length. The electrical system went out. Sigsbee's cabin was plunged into darkness. Choking smoke filled the room.

Outside, there was anything but darkness. The night air was split by a dazzling light that accompanied the second explosion. It stunned two men, Louis Werthheimer and Sigmond Rothschild, who were seated in deck chairs on an American liner, the *City of Washington*, anchored more than a 100 yards (91 meters) away. Aghast, they saw smoke and flame boil 150 feet (46 meters) into the air, twisting into a cloud that spread away to all sides. Out of the churning red and black mass came a rain of bodies and chunks of metal. Some landed in the water half a mile from the stricken ship.

Aboard the *Maine*, the enlisted men were housed in the forecastle, an area up forward by the ship's bow. Below them was a storage place for ammunition, called a magazine, where between 8 and 10 tons of gun powder were stored. The explosions occurred next to the magazine, causing the men in the forecastle to take the full force of the two blasts.

Most were killed instantly, their bodies ripped apart and flung out into the night. Others survived, but were crushed in their bunks under tons of debris. They were drowned in the water that burst through the torn hull. (The space between some decks after the blast was just a few inches or even less.) Fewer than six managed to escape the wreckage. All six were hurt, covered with blood and black with smoke and burns.

Sailors elsewhere on the ship fared better. One man who had bedded down in his gun turret was jolted awake and instantly hurled into the sea. Two sailors standing near the stern heard the "shotgun" blast and then felt themselves falling as the deck beneath them split open. A moment later, they were lying in the darkness below, pinned beneath heavy wreckage. Then came the second blast. It tore the wreckage away from them. They quickly clamored back topside.

Lieutenants John Hood and John Blandin, the two officers who were seated near the stern as they smoked their last cigars of the day, escaped serious injury but were given a frightening view of the disaster. When Hood heard the "gunshot," he looked toward the bow just in time for the second explosion. He saw "the whole starboard side of the deck and everything . . .

spring into the air with all kinds of objects in it . . . with flames and everything else coming up." A piece of flying debris knocked the lieutenant's cap off. Unharmed, he dashed toward the stern so that he could organize a party to lower the ship's boats.

Blandin likewise looked toward the bow at the first sign of trouble. He later wrote that, in the wake of the second blast, "a perfect rain of missiles of all descriptions, from huge pieces of cement to blocks of wood, steel railings, and fragments of gratings" came raining down on the deck. A piece of cement knocked him off his feet. Only slightly hurt, he raced after Hood to help with the boats.

Dazed and choking, Captain Sigsbee staggered out of his cabin and made his way outside to the starboard deck. The sight that greeted him there stunned him anew. Ammunition was being hurled from the fiery magazine and exploding overhead, creating a deadly fireworks display. Bodies were floating in the water, the living among them yelling for help. Up forward, there was a mountain of twisted metal and wood that had once been the deck and the quarters below it. One of the twin stacks had toppled and now lay across the starboard deck, angling into the water.

Over on the *City of Washington*, lifeboats went into the water with a crash and began making their way to the Americans in the water. The rescue effort was joined by boats from a nearby Spanish warship—the cruiser *Alfonso XII*. All the boats made their way to the struggling figures and hurriedly, but gently, lifted them to safety. All the while, they ignored the debris raining down on them from the ammunition exploding overhead and creating the ghastly fireworks display that brought Carnival on the shore to a halt. Hundreds of celebrants stopped and gaped at the harbor sky.

As soon as Captain Sigsbee came on deck, he ordered boats over the side to fetch the men from the water. Then, struck with the thought that the explosions might be the signal for an attack on his ship, he called for guards to be stationed along the rail to ward off any attackers. He canceled the order moments later when he realized that the blazing *Maine* would be of no use to any enemy. There was no way of putting out the fire; every piece of firefighting gear had been destroyed. Even if water could be poured on the flames, the ship could not be saved. It was going down too fast. Already, the harbor water was almost up to deck level.

His voice hoarse, he gave the order to abandon ship, then watched his remaining crewmen swing their legs over the ship's rail and drop into the boats that rocked alongside. The captain remained standing where he was until certain that all the men had left. Then, in accordance with nautical tradition the world over, he became the last man to leave his ship.

The *Maine* burned for hours after the last of its bursting ammunition had stained the night sky. By dawn on February 16, all that was left of the once proud ship was a smoldering hulk lying on the floor of the shallow bay with nothing but its forward mast and the twisted wreckage above its deck visible to the eye.

On all counts, the loss of the *Maine* was a major disaster for the United States. Of the ship's 343 enlisted men and 31 officers, 260 were dead (252 were killed outright, with eight dying later). The nation had lost a fine ship—a loss that was to plunge the country into its final conflict of the nineteenth century, which had been marked by the War of 1812, the Mexican War, the Civil War, and the Indian Wars. Now to burst on the scene was the Spanish-American War.

Chapter 2—The Roots of War

How did the death of the *Maine* lead to war with Spain? The answer can be found in the history of Spanish rule in Cuba. It was a rule that began when Columbus came upon the island during his 1492 voyage and claimed it in the name of Spain. Over the centuries, it proved to be a brutal and dictatorial rule that decimated the original Indian population and then drove the Cuban people to rebellion three and a half centuries later. Making matters worse for the Cubans were the diseases—among them smallpox and cholera—that the Europeans brought to the island. The Cubans finally rose against their Spanish masters in 1868.

The uprising was the latest in a series of New World troubles for Spain. Once a major power there, it was now aged and weak. It had lost one holding after another in the 1800s as their subject people had successfully fought for their freedom. Among the nations newly independent from Spain were Colombia, Venezuela, Bolivia, Peru, and Mexico.

Now the people of Cuba—especially its African slaves, freed slaves, and Haitian immigrants—were to seek their freedom. They battled courageously with

The *Virginius* Crisis

Despite the American effort to remain on good terms with Spain during the Ten Years' War, the two countries once ran into a problem that brought them to the brink of war. It happened in 1873.

Causing the trouble was the *Virginius*, a small iron freighter that was captured by a Spanish gunboat while smuggling arms to the Cuban rebels. At the time, the freighter was flying an American flag and captained by an American, Joseph Fry. There was, however, a question whether the ship was actually American-owned. It was a question that was never answered.

Nor was it a question that bothered the Spanish authorities in Cuba. Once captured, the *Virginius* was taken to the port city of Santiago de Cuba. There, its officers, crewmen, and passengers—208 men in all—were tried for piracy and quickly judged guilty. Then, over a five-day period, 53 of their number, including Fry, were executed by a firing squad. Some of the corpses were decapitated and the heads mounted on pikes for public display.

There was an outraged cry in America over the brutal punishment, no matter that the *Virginius* had been illegally running guns. The U.S. Navy mobilized for action and prepared to send a small flotilla against the Spanish in Cuba. But Hamilton Fish, secretary of state under President Ulysses S. Grant, held the flotilla in check. He knew that the operation would fail. The United States, still recovering from the Civil War, could not muster enough ships for a successful assault even against a foe as weak as Spain.

Still alive and awaiting execution at Santiago were 155 men. All but 12 of their number were spared when a British gunboat docked at the city and its captain objected so vehemently to the savage outcome of the trial that the government in Spain canceled the remaining executions. The crisis came to a close when Spain apologized for the incident and paid $80,000 to the families of the executed men.

Spanish troops in what became known as the "Ten Years' War" before finally being subdued. All the while, many Americans watched the Cuban struggle with sympathy, comparing it to their own revolution a century earlier.

Regardless of public opinion, the U.S. government did not support the uprising during the years of fighting. America, with virtually no navy to battle an overseas power, had no wish for trouble with Spain, even knowing how weak the once-powerful nation had become.

When the Ten Years' War ended in defeat for the rebels in 1878, there followed a new period of harsh Spanish rule. The Cubans were shackled with taxes to support a Spanish army of occupation and a corrupt Spanish bureaucracy. Making matters worse were commercial regulations that favored Spain and raised havoc with the local economy. A devastating economic depression hit the island in the 1890s. It was more than the people could bear. Revolution flamed again, this time in 1895.

THE NEW REBELLION

The new outbreak was fought by an army of 25,000 to 30,000 Cubans from all walks of life—from peasants to teachers and intellectuals. They waged a savage guerrilla war, attacking and burning sugar plantations in various areas of the island, ambushing army units wherever they found them, and raiding enemy military posts everywhere. They hoped to be rid of the hated overlords by destroying the island's economy and starving their army into surrender. They also hoped that the attacks on the plantations, many of which were owned by Americans, would draw the United States into the conflict to defend its interests and defeat the Spanish. Their efforts were so successful that Spain had to commit 150,000 troops to the fighting.

This etching, published in Harper's Weekly *in June 1896, shows the Cuban rebels behind their well-guarded, fortified fences. The appearance of this image in what was a popular newsmagazine of the time indicates an interest by the general public before the fever pitch that was reached once Pulitzer and Hearst started headlining the conflict.*

The Spanish and Cubans battled for a year. Both sides laid waste to the land and slaughtered their prisoners—all to no avail. Finally, the government in Madrid tried to win the upper hand by sending a new governor to the island, General Valeriano Weyler y Nicolau. Known as an able soldier, he arrived with fresh troops and immediately surrounded the rebel areas of activity with barbed-wire entanglements, trenches, and armed blockhouses. He then embarked on a cruel strategy that spelled death for thousands of innocent Cubans.

Called *reconcentrado*, meaning reconcentration, the strategy was meant to keep the peasant population from joining the revolution. Weyler ordered all the men, women, and children living in rural areas to report to nearby Spanish garrisons; anyone who failed to obey would be put on trial as a traitor. On arrival, the people were herded into hastily built detention camps that were without adequate food and decent sanitation facilities. Starvation and disease quickly took a terrible toll. It was estimated that, of the 400,000 people imprisoned, between 95,000 and 200,000 perished.

Until they heard of *reconcentrado*, the American people had sympathized with the Cubans. Now their sympathy flamed into outrage. The Spanish were beasts and the island people helpless victims. Suddenly, Americans everywhere were demanding that Washington, D.C., intervene and put a stop to the cruelty, even if it meant risking war with Spain.

It should be noted that the Cuban rebels had a policy similar to *reconcentrado*. With it, they threatened to kill peasants who worked on the foreign-owned plantations. Many peasants then lost their lives when they were faced with trying to go to work or starving.

THE DEMANDS FOR INTERVENTION

The initial U.S. demand, a humanitarian cry, was joined by others. One was economic in nature. About $50 million in U.S. capital was invested in Cuba, mainly in the sugarcane industry. Further, the nation's trade with Cuba prior to the rebellion had come to $100 million a year. Washington had to put an end to the trouble before it severely damaged the American economy.

A recent change in the view that many Americans held of their country was behind yet another demand. Throughout the 1800s, the nation had expanded under the banner of Manifest Destiny—the widespread belief that its people were duty-bound to extend its borders from the Atlantic to the Pacific and from Canada south to Mexico. That goal had now been won, and there was a New Manifest Destiny spreading through the land—the desire to turn the United States into a world power, both commercially and militarily.

There were several reasons behind this desire. The country was successfully recovering from the Civil War which had ended in 1865. Its east and west coasts were now linked by railroad tracks, as were cities throughout the country. The population had grown mightily. So had the nation's businesses, both at home and abroad. Overseas, along with their investments in Cuba, U.S. companies had now put $151 million into European enterprises and $200 million into Mexican concerns.

It would later be said by many that the United States became a world power because of the Spanish-American War. This was true, but only partly so. With its overseas investments, the nation was already on the road to becoming an economic giant internationally when the fighting began with Spain.

Further, the United States had secured the rights to build coaling and maintenance stations on two Pacific islands for naval and commercial ventures in Asia—Samoa in 1878 and Hawaii (for the base at Pearl Harbor) in 1887.

In all, America was bursting at the seams, ripe to expand outward and truly become a major world power in the coming twentieth century. And there were national leaders—among them the young assistant secretary of the navy, Theodore Roosevelt—who stood ready to whip the expansion along by going to war and driving Spain out of the Caribbean. Spain's departure would also be a major triumph for the Monroe Doctrine. Ever since 1823, it had held that the New World was no longer to be a target of foreign colonization.

All the public anger over the Cuban problem led Congress to call for President Grover Cleveland to prod Spain into acknowledging the island's independence. Cleveland, however, refused to act. He believed that any attempt to have Spain toss away its remaining major colony in the New World would lead to war. No matter that Spain was a mere shadow of its former self, he had no desire for war with the country.

Neither did his successor, William McKinley, who was elected to the White House in 1896. Though flooded with demands for action against Spain, he refused to behave impetuously. Instead, he began talking with the Spanish leaders to find a peaceful solution to the problem, one that would somehow please both sides. Possibilities included limited home rule for Cuba, plus various economic and agricultural reforms.

HEARST, PULITZER, AND "YELLOW JOURNALISM"

Two influential men made McKinley's work especially difficult. They were newspaper publishers William Randolph Hearst and Joseph Pulitzer. Both—Hearst with his *New York Evening Journal* and Pulitzer with his *New York World*—practiced a new form of news reportage that was attracting an ever-widening readership. Called "yellow journalism," it featured bold headlines and the coverage of sensational topics (sex,

William Randolph Hearst

Joseph Pulitzer

scandals, and lurid human-interest stories), writing of them all in a punchy and fast-paced style. For example, when Pulitzer's *World* once ran the story of a heat wave that killed 400 infants, it headlined the report "HOW BABIES ARE BAKED." Hearst's *Evening Journal* gave Spain's General Weyler the nickname by which he became known throughout the United States: "The Butcher."

The term "yellow journalism" took its name from a cartoon character called "The Yellow Kid of Hogan's Alley." Drawn by Richard Outcault and colored yellow by means of a new printing process, the character—a big-eared slum child—first appeared on the front page of Pulitzer's *World*. Later, when Hearst lured Outcault away from the *World*, Pulitzer hired a new cartoonist and the Kid became a feature in both papers.

Using yellow journalism as their chief weapon, Hearst and Pulitzer were fighting a war to win the greatest number of readers in New York, America's biggest city and a prize for any publisher with its 3 million people. Their main battleground became the Cuban revolution, a subject that, bathed in violence,

This etching from Pulitzer's New York World *shows an unbelievably hateful looking man representing Spain and a starved woman representing Cuba. This type of image inflamed readers.*

Yellow Journalism: How False? How True?

Much of the material printed by Hearst and Pulitzer was provided by a group of Cuban patriots who settled in New York City and whose job it was to spread anti-Spanish propaganda among the Americans and raise money for the revolutionary cause. The two publishers took full advantage of the sensational propaganda, regardless of whether or not it was true, and then invented horror stories of their own when needed.

For example, when the noted artist Frederic Remington went to Cuba to draw illustrations for the *New York Evening Journal*, he delighted Hearst by sending a sketch of male Spanish customs officers removing an American woman's clothing in a search for hidden contraband. The illustration was a figment of Remington's imagination because the actual search had been conducted by women officers. But the picture and an accompanying story shocked the *Journal*'s readers and filled them with disgust for Spain. They did not know—nor did the newspaper tell them—that Spanish customs searches of women were always conducted by female officers.

Fortunately, not all newspapers handled the Cuban rebellion in an irresponsible manner. But unfortunately, many papers across the country did turn to yellow journalism when they learned of the fortunes being reaped by Hearst and Pulitzer.

In fairness, it must be said that not all of yellow journalism's reportage was false. In one of the best-known stories of the prewar weeks, Hearst's *Journal* printed a letter revealing the behind-the-scenes

was sure to attract all types of readers. Each man, knowing the sympathies of the American people, made the Spanish the villains in their reporting and tried to outdo the other with horror stories of Spanish cruelties, as witness this blood-soaked report in Pulitzer's *World*:

> The horrors of a barbarous struggle for the extermination of the native population are witnessed in all parts of the country. Blood on the roadsides, blood on the fields, blood on the doorsteps, blood, blood, blood!

Reporters in the field

lacking in good faith in his dealings with Spain and branded him a weakling. The letter had been sent to a Spanish newspaper editor but was thought to have then been stolen by some Cuban supporter and forwarded to the *Journal*.

As expected, Americans everywhere greeted the letter with white-hot rage. How dare a foreigner call their president a weakling, even though many of their own kind had branded him "Wobbly Willie"? For a week or two, the letter was a major topic of infuriated conversation, and nothing could cool the American tempers, not even the minister's quick resignation and Spain's apology. Then it was abruptly swept off the front pages by the news of the *Maine* disaster.

opinion of a Spanish diplomat. Written by Enrique Dupuy du Lome, the Spanish minister to Washington, the letter accused President McKinley of

As a result of such reporting, the public anger against Spain mounted throughout 1897, even though there was talk that, due to President McKinley's negotiations, Spain might soon grant the Cubans a degree of self-government.

But that talk triggered another anger—this one among the Spaniards living in Cuba. To them, the idea of a self-governing Cuba was so loathsome that it prodded them into several weeks of rioting in Havana.

It was because of these riots that the *Maine* was sent to Havana in early 1898. Its task—to protect the Americans living there and to remove them to safety if necessary—ended in tragedy on that terrible night of February 15.

WAR FEVER

William Randolph Hearst received word of the explosions from one of his *Evening Journal* editors late that night. He had one terse reaction: "This means war."

His prediction was to come true within two months. The cause of the explosion was unknown, but that did not matter to the American public. Thanks much to the one-sided reporting in the yellow press, people everywhere were certain that the Spanish government had somehow sabotaged the ship. There was an immediate demand that Washington take action against Spain to avenge the deaths of 260 fine servicemen. Suddenly echoing across the country was the battle cry:

Remember the *Maine*!
To hell with Spain!

Two investigations were launched into the cause of the explosions—one conducted by the U.S. Navy, and the other by the Spanish government. When completed in March, they offered opposing views of the disaster. From the blown-inward condition of the metal in the area of the blasts, the navy held that they had been triggered by a force outside the ship: Either the *Maine* had been accidentally struck by a mine that the Spanish had placed for defensive purposes in the harbor or had been blown apart by one that divers had deliberately attached to the hull.

The Spanish government held that the explosions had occurred on the inside and had been likely caused by a fire. (This view was supported by a U.S. study in 1976 that decided there had been an accidental explosion caused by a fire in a coal bunker next to a magazine.)

The mystery of who or what caused the explosions was never fully solved. To Americans everywhere, however, the navy study justified their suspicions of Spanish villainy. The Madrid government was at fault. No doubt about it.

But was there merit to these suspicions? Spain was an old and weak country. Would it dare do anything that would certainly trigger a war with the young and vigorous United States? For many historians, the answer has always been "no." Surely, they have argued, Spain wanted no such conflict. And was it not possible that the Cubans themselves had triggered the explosion—all for the purpose of drawing the United States into a war with Spain?

For his part, President McKinley wanted no war with the Spanish, no matter how aged and weak their country might be. He had fought for the Union in the Civil War and had seen enough bloodshed to last him a lifetime. Further, he feared that a war would disrupt his nation's economic life. He insisted on trying to reach a peaceful Cuban settlement, even though it won him the scorn of many Americans and the nickname "Wobbly Willie."

Cautious though he was, McKinley was not a man of infinite patience. He finally had enough of the Spanish by the start of April. In late March he had sent them a new plan for Cuba. They accepted it in part, but balked on several key issues, especially the all-important demand that Spain promise to grant Cuba its independence.

President McKinley at his desk in 1898.

Angered at this latest stumbling block, McKinley sent a message to Congress on April 11, calling for U.S. intervention to liberate Cuba and its people. Congress replied with a joint resolution on April 19. The resolution proclaimed Cuba an independent nation and authorized the president to take whatever steps he deemed necessary to drive the Spanish out.

With the resolution in hand, McKinley ordered a navy squadron out to blockade the Cuban coast and

The Teller Amendment

The congressional resolution of April 19 contained a significant amendment by Senator Henry M. Teller of Colorado. It specified that the United States had no intention of exercising any "sovereignty, jurisdiction, or control" over Cuba once the Spanish had been ousted.

All that the nation intended to do, instead, was to restore peace to Cuba and then "leave the government and control of the island to its people."

The Teller Amendment was a promise not to annex Cuba and make it a U.S. holding once the war was won and it was enthusiastically greeted by everyone who favored the New Manifest Destiny but did not want the nation to take control of any country and become a colonial power like Great Britain, Russia, or Germany. All that it desired were coaling stations for its military and commercial shipping, such as those that had been secured in Samoa and the Hawaiian Islands. The amendment could leave no doubt that America was helping Cuba not for selfish but for humanitarian reasons.

But the amendment was also a cause for concern among many Americans. They feared that the promise to depart Cuba would keep the United States. from taking action should the island's various political factions begin fighting each other for power once the Spanish left. Civil strife had followed the struggles for freedom in other of the newly independent South American and Caribbean nations and could happen again—this time very close to home.

cut off the flow of military aid from Spain. Then, on April 24, the Spanish declared war on the United States. Congress replied with a declaration of its own the next day, saying that a state of hostilities had existed with Spain since April 21.

America at last was at war.

Chapter 3—Girding for Action

The United States began the war in what struck many Americans as an odd place. The conflict had been brought on by events in Cuba, but it opened with a battle fought thousands of miles to the west, far beyond the Caribbean and clear across the Pacific, in the Philippine Islands.

The battle was waged in giant Manila Bay, which lay on the southwest coast of Luzon, the largest of the more than 7,000 islands of the Philippines. Its waters washed up on the capital city of Manila.

Explorer Ferdinand Magellan had come upon the islands in 1521 during his round-the-world voyage and had claimed them for Spain. The Spanish began colonizing them in 1565 and named them in honor of King Philip II. From then on, they served as Spain's principal holding in the far Pacific. Then, in 1895, they became a target of the U.S. Navy.

Between 1895 and 1897, Navy planners decided that the United States must take Manila Bay and the city of Manila if the Cuban trouble exploded into war. There were two reasons behind the decision. First, much of the Spanish navy was stationed at Manila; when the bay fell to the Americans, the enemy ships would be trapped and unable to join the fighting in Cuba or launch an attack against the American west coast. Second, Manila was a major port through which tons of Spanish goods flowed to the world. That flow would be cut off and further weaken the already weak Spain.

By the dawn of 1898, the navy realized that war was inevitable and began preparing for its arrival. In February, the Navy Department cabled all commanders with instructions to ready their units for the outbreak of fighting. The cables were sent by Theodore Roosevelt, the energetic assistant secretary of the navy. He was temporarily filling in for his superior, Secretary John D. Long, who was in poor health and away from his office.

At the same time, Roosevelt dispatched a special message to Commodore George Dewey, the newly appointed commander of the Asiatic Squadron, the nation's fleet in the far Pacific. He ordered the sixty-one-year-old Dewey to assemble his ships at the British colony of Hong Kong. There, he would take on supplies and coal and await orders for the move against Manila Bay, just 600 miles (966 kilometers) away.

A brilliant officer and a graduate of the Naval Academy in 1855, Dewey had

Commodore Dewey in 1898

Two officers were chiefly responsible for the strength of the United States at sea in the 1890s—Rear Admiral Steven B. Luce and Captain Alfred Thayer Mahan.

Both men insisted that the nation required a vastly improved navy and merchant marine as it approached the 1900s and the greatness that the new century promised. Admiral Luce urged that the men in both services be better trained and that America establish a college for officers. His advice bore fruit when the Naval War College was founded in 1884. The admiral was named as its first president.

Luce then brought Captain Mahan—a fellow visionary—to the War College faculty. There, Mahan argued, if the nation hoped to have a successful merchant fleet, it must have a powerful navy to defend the commercial vessels from attack. The additional benefit would be a navy which could defend America's shores from attack and then go on the offensive itself.

For both these tasks, the navy must develop large ships with giant coal bunkers so that they could carry sufficient fuel for extensive periods at sea and voyages to the far reaches of the world. To provide the needed fuel, the navy must maintain coaling stations (such as those at Samoa and Hawaii) at points all around the globe—points that could be reached as quickly as possible whenever fuel ran short.

Mahan wrote two textbooks on naval power and strategies. They became required reading for the officers of nations across the world. The captain later served as president of the War College.

served under Admiral David Farragut during the Civil War, sailing on the admiral's successful expedition against the Confederacy's holdings along the Mississippi River. Roosevelt handed him the Asiatic Squadron because he was a resourceful officer who could wage a successful campaign, even though halfway around the world from his home base. He was just the sort of man that the tough Roosevelt liked.

It was fitting that the navy should fight the first battle of the war. The sea service was far better equipped for the job than the army. Ever since the end of the Civil War, the federal government in Washington, D.C., had allowed the army to dwindle away to just over 28,000 officers and men. They were well trained but too small a force and too poorly equipped for a major conflict. Time would be needed to increase the army's size, train the recruits, and equip the troops with sufficient arms before ever going into battle.

The navy had also been allowed to fall into disrepair following the Civil War. But it was now in fighting trim because, in the previous decade, Congress had invested heavily in a shipbuilding program while high-ranking officers had concentrated on improving the training of all personnel. Both the construction and training programs were born of the New Manifest Destiny, with its aim of making the United States an international power. As a result, along with its older vessels, the navy presently boasted seven of the most modern warships afloat.

DEWEY AT HONG KONG

On taking over the Asiatic Squadron, Dewey made his headquarters at Nagasaki, Japan. But by the time he was told to gather his squadron at Hong Kong, he had already moved there, making the shift because he knew that he would soon be called upon to strike in the Philippines. He had sailed his flagship, the cruiser *Olympia*, into Hong Kong harbor on February 17, two days after the *Maine* had been destroyed at Havana.

Now, on Roosevelt's orders, he summoned the ships of his squadron to his side from their various stations, among them, Korea, China, Japan, and the Mediterranean Sea. In the next weeks, eight vessels steamed into Hong Kong harbor. Of that number, six were warships. The *Olympia* was joined by three fellow cruisers (the *Boston*, *Raleigh*, and *Baltimore)*, two gunboats (the *Petrel* and *Concord*), and a speedy revenue cutter (the *Hugh McCulloch*). In addition, there were two commercial vessels—one a freighter to provide the warships with supplies, and the other a collier to feed them coal. Manning the fleet was a force of 1,748 seamen and marines.

The Petrel, *coming into Hong Kong harbor in 1898.*
Notice the other American vessels in the background.
They were all gathering to be prepared for war.

The warships were splendid things to see as they glided into port. They were painted with the navy's glistening peacetime white and fitted with highly polished brasswork and gleaming wood paneling. Dewey immediately set about preparing them for combat. A gray-green paint was spread over their hulls and superstructures. The interior wood paneling that could easily catch fire in battle began to be removed; the job would be completed during the voyage to the Philippines. Each ship went into drydock for a bottom scraping in order to increase its speed at sea.

Fine as his ships looked, Dewey faced three problems at Hong Kong. First, the squadron was smaller than he wished it to be. Though well equipped, the Navy could not give him all the ships he wanted for a major campaign. Too many were needed for the blockade of Cuba.

Next, his ships were always in need of coal, which they burned by the ton for their boilers. Dewey purchased as much of the fuel as possible in Hong Kong, but there was never as much as he needed, inasmuch as the port was heavily used by the navies of the European nations that were competing for power in China—Great Britain itself, Germany, Russia, and Japan. All were clamoring for coal.

Finally, the commodore had yet to receive all the ammunition needed for the Philippine attack. It was for this reason that the cruiser *Baltimore* gave him some especially bad moments. The vessel had been transferred to his squadron from duty at Hawaii and was now sailing to Hong Kong with ammunition for the Philippines campaign.

Dewey feared that war would erupt before the *Baltimore* arrived. Hong Kong was a British colony. When hostilities broke out, Great Britain would insist that the rules of neutrality for nations not engaged in the fighting be observed in all its holdings. Dewey would be ordered to leave in the name of Britain's neutrality and would have to put to sea without sufficient ammunition. Precious time would then be lost in meeting the *Baltimore* elsewhere.

On Friday, April 22, the news came that the United States and Spain had severed diplomatic relations and that war was only hours away. The next day, April 23, Hong Kong's governor-general notified Dewey that the American fleet must clear the harbor by 4:00 P.M. on the coming Monday, April 25. The governor-general told Dewey that he personally regretted giving the order.

The *Baltimore* finally made her way into the harbor on April 22. Small boats sped to its side, removed its ammunition stores, and distributed them throughout the squadron. Then the ship was pulled out of the water to be scraped and painted over with battle gray-green. Sweating round the clock, sailors and dock workers finished the job in a mere 48 hours. Much to the amazement of the foreign crews in port, the cruiser was back in the water on April 25.

The squadron departed at 9:30 A.M. Dewey had not yet received final orders from the Navy Department to move against Manila Bay, so he traveled only 30 miles (48 kilometers) south through the South China Sea and dropped anchor at a small, deserted harbor on the China coast. There, he awaited the arrival of word from the Navy Department.

That word reached Hong Kong just two hours after his departure. Ensign Harry Caldwell, a young officer who had remained behind to receive the expected message, quickly boarded a chartered tug and hurried to Dewey. When the commodore opened the message, he read:

> War has commenced between the United States and Spain. Proceed at once to Philippine Islands. Commence operations at once, particularly against the Spanish fleet. You must capture or destroy. Use utmost endeavor.

The message was signed by John D. Long, the secretary of the navy.

Dewey spent Tuesday, April 26, making final preparations for the voyage to Manila Bay. His men also devoted hours to gunnery practice and fire and damage control. Then, early on April 27, the squadron set out to sea following a course southeast to the island of Luzon. The time for battle had come.

By Saturday, April 30, Dewey was sailing down the west coast of Luzon. At dawn that day, he sighted the mouth of Subic Bay, a few miles to the north of Manila Bay. He sent the *Baltimore*, *Boston*, and *Concord* into the bay to see if any enemy ships were lurking in its waters. The Spanish were surely aware of his approach and had possibly hidden a force there to strike him from the rear when he entered Manila Bay. If so, it had to be destroyed.

The three warships, after probing all corners of the bay, returned to the open sea in the mid-afternoon, with the *Concord* flashing the message "Nothing in sight." A jubilant Dewey summoned his captains to the *Olympia* and told them that they would enter Manila Bay that night and, as one officer remembered the commodore's words: "Engage the enemy forces should they be found."

INTO MANILA BAY

At 11:30 P.M., Dewey made out the entrance to the giant bay, which measured 775 square miles (2,007 square kilometers) and boasted a shoreline of more than 100 miles (160 kilometers). Near its northeast corner lay the city of Manila, with a population of 300,000.

About 12 miles (19 kilometers) to the southwest, the bay became two smaller bodies of water one after the other—first, Cañacao Bay and then Bacoor Bay. Jutting out between the two was a narrow peninsula on which was located the Cavite naval base, the home of Spain's Philippine fleet.

Looming in the entrance to Manila Bay was the island of Corregidor, with two channels sweeping past it—Boca Chica (Little Mouth) on its north side and Boca Grande (Big Mouth) on the south. Dewey led his ships into Boca Grande and had advanced but a short distance when a rocket suddenly shot high above Corregidor, briefly turning the night into whitish day. A sharp intake of breath went through the squadron. His 1,748 men knew that they had been sighted. The Spanish on Corregidor caught a glimpse of the American force when the soot in the *McCulloch*'s smokestack burst into flames and burned brightly for a short while.

A moment later, a cannon roared on El Fraile (The Friar), a rocky outcrop in Boca Grande. A shell exploded in the water between the cruiser *Raleigh* and the gunboat *Petrel*. It sent a geyser of water spurting high but did no damage. The squadron, lobbing a few shells at the Spanish defenses, sailed past El Fraile and into the bay's open waters.

Dewey at once set his course for Manila, some 30 miles (48 kilometers) ahead, reducing his speed to 4 knots (7,408 meters, or 24,304 feet) so that he would reach the city at dawn. At 4:00 A.M. the crews ate a meal of bread, beans, and coffee before taking their battle stations. As daylight began to spread over the bay, Dewey could make out the Manila breakwater in

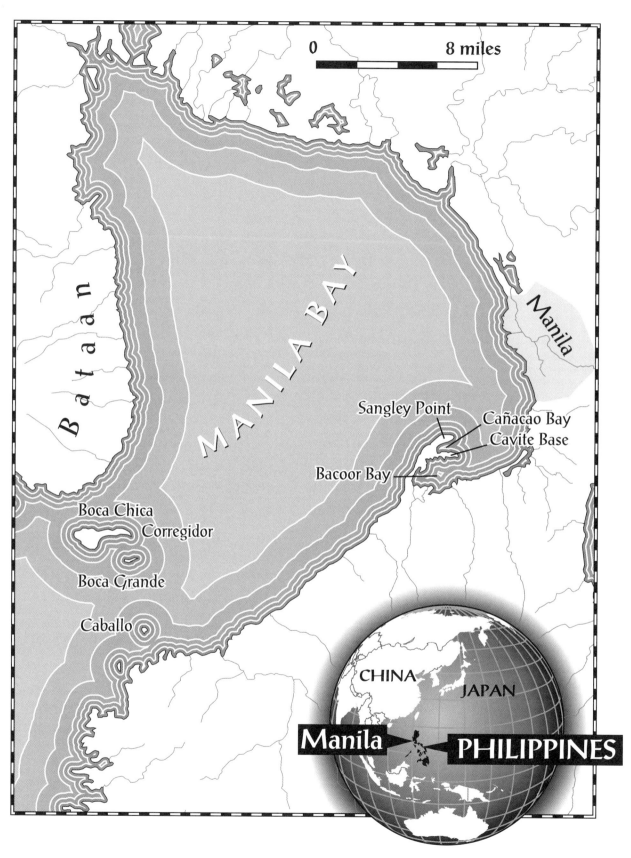

0   8 miles

B a t a a n

MANILA BAY

Manila

Sangley Point

Cañacao Bay

Cavite Base

Bacoor Bay

Boca Chica

Corregidor

Boca Grande

Caballo

CHINA

JAPAN

Manila ► ◄ PHILIPPINES

his glass. It stood about 6 miles (10 kilometers) away, with ships crowding the docks behind it. He had expected to see Spanish warships waiting for him in the shadow of the shore batteries guarding the city. But not a single fighting ship was to be seen.

Where was the enemy fleet? It was thought to be here, but it was not drawn up in front of the city. Nor had it moved to Subic Bay. So where was it? Dewy got his answer when he swung his glass southward. He made out the shapes of seven Spanish warships in Cañacao Bay. They rode at anchor in a curving line just north of the peninsula that housed the Cavite base, and just off a tip of land known as Sangley Point. They were about 6 miles (10 kilometers) away, with smaller ships clustered behind and around them. The commodore quickly sensed why the commander of the Philippine fleet, Rear Admiral Patricio Montojo, had chosen to fight at Cavite: He hoped to keep the invaders from bombarding Manila.

Dewey was now three miles from the Manila breakwater. He ordered a sharp turn to starboard. The squadron swung smartly south in a single file, with the *Olympia* leading and with its sister ships following at 400-yard (366-meter) intervals.

Soon after the turn, the more than 200 guns (a mixture of modern and obsolete pieces) defending Manila opened fire. The first of their shells hit just astern of the *Baltimore* but did no harm. Nor did the rest of the shells that came hurtling in from the batteries lining the shore south toward Cañacao Bay, their failure caused by poor marksmanship.

At a little after 5:00 A.M., a new thunder joined the thump of the shore batteries. The guns on Sangley Point and at Cavite's Fort San Felipe now began to fire at the oncoming Americans. The first shots fell short

An Overmatched Enemy

Admiral Montojo commanded more ships than did Dewey, and he was fighting on his own home ground when they met on that fateful May 1. But on two counts he was far outclassed by the American force.

First, every one of his ships— the *Reina Cristina*, *Castilla*, *Don Juan de Austria*, *Luzon*, *Cuba*, *Duero*, and *Don Antonio Ulloa*— was aged and fitted with obsolete equipment. Dewey's ships, even the older ones, were better equipped than anything that the Spanish admiral had at hand.

There was another critical difference between the two forces. It was to be seen in their respective commanders. Dewey exuded confidence and was ready to win. Montojo recognized the inferiority of his fleet and felt that he had no chance of victory. Yet he went on serving loyally, anchoring his defensive line in the shallows off Cavite so that Dewey would be lured away from the city of Manila and spare it a shelling.

Dewey's confidence in himself and his squadron was not shared by the naval officers of the several nations whose ships were anchored around him at Hong Kong. Though fully aware of Spain's fading glory on the international scene, they thought that the Spanish navy still had the strength to defeat the U.S. squadron. After all, at that time, the American navy had yet to fight a battle and its gunners had yet to prove that they were good at their jobs.

Dewey's officers, when visiting officers aboard the foreign ships, found that it was impossible to get anyone to bet on an American victory. One British officer, after a dinner given for Dewey's officers, looked at the departing guests and told his friends: "A fine set of fellows, but unhappily we shall never see them again."

and wide of their targets, with those that followed describing wild and harmless patterns. A smiling Dewey told his staff officers, "Evidently the Spanish are already rattled." He was right.

The Americans did not immediately answer the fire. Rather, the squadron continued to plough relentlessly toward the enemy fleet. Dewey was holding back his shots until he was sure that they would hit their targets. With each passing moment, he could see the seven Spanish warships more clearly. The cheers of their crews echoed across the water as, on Admiral Montojo's order, Spain's traditional battle flags of crimson and gold rose to the mastheads. On seeing them the American crewmen began shouting, "Remember the *Maine*!"

THE PARADE OF DEATH

At 5:15 A.M., the Spanish ships opened fire. Dewey held his course until he was about 5,000 yards (4,572 meters) off Cavite. Then he passed a simple order to Captain Charles V. Gridley, the skipper of the *Olympia*. When news of it reached home, it was proudly echoed everywhere and won a place in the nation's history: "You may fire when you are ready, Gridley."

The order sent signal flags up the *Olympia*'s masthead, where they snapped out flat in the wind with the message "Engage the enemy."

The bombardment began with an 8-inch (203-millimeter) shell from the *Olympia*. Then, on Dewey's order, the squadron swung to the west, turning its portside guns toward the Spanish fleet. As one, the U.S. guns opened a furious broadside barrage. After a short westward sail, the squadron swung about and began to march back and forth past the enemy line, wreaking terrible havoc with every pass. The march was to take Dewey sweeping past the Spaniards several times—five times as he sailed west, and four as he returned east.

Not an enemy vessel escaped devastating harm. One warship, ripped apart by a series of direct hits,

In this 1898 print the Olympia, *in the foreground, and her sister vessels handily lay waste to virtually the entire Spanish defensive fleet.*

caught fire and had to be scuttled. Another ship lost all but two of its guns and was struck by a shell that wounded half the crew. Still another was rendered helpless with the loss of three guns, and yet another with the loss of all but one battery.

The worst damage befell the *Reina Cristina*, Admiral Montojo's flagship. With his fleet being mauled and with his own decks ablaze, he had the

Reina Cristina break ranks and attack the *Olympia*. It was a desperate attempt to change the course of battle by crippling the U.S. flagship.

The effort cost the *Reina Cristina* its life. A rain of shells from the *Olympia*'s rapid-fire guns destroyed its steam-powered steering system and riddled the forward smokestack with so many holes that it came crashing down. One shell hit the stern and killed nine men in an instant. Others shot away the top of the mizzenmast. The ship's sick bay took a direct hit, with all the wounded there losing their lives. In total, more than 150 of Montojo's 352 crewmen and officers were killed or wounded by the shelling.

The crew, however, fought on courageously until a shell triggered a fire in one of the *Reina Cristina*'s magazines. Before the flames could cause all the ammunition on board to explode, Montojo signaled for two ships to come alongside and take the remnants of his crew to safety. He then went over the side and was carried back to his blazing fleet. The *Reina Cristina* drifted toward shore and sank to its main deck in the shallows.

Dewey's squadron did not escape without a scar during the parade of death. The Spanish gunners, though trapped in choking smoke, unleashed hundreds of shells in the hours of fighting. But most fell short or wide of their targets by at least a ship's length. They managed to shower the U.S. vessels with steel fragments that ripped holes in ships' boats, tore rigging ropes to shreds, and left pockmarks in hulls, decks, and superstructures, all without doing any serious harm.

The *Baltimore* suffered the worst damage when a 4.7-inch (1.194-millimeter) shell struck on the starboard side and smashed through the hull. It then hurtled along an interior deck, bouncing off various surfaces until it sailed back outside through an open hatch. It slammed into—and crippled—a 6-inch (152-millimeter) gun before it ended its wild journey by crashing into a box of rapid-fire shells. Some of their number exploded, flinging shrapnel in all directions and slightly wounding eight men—the only Americans to be harmed that day. The *Baltimore*, however, remained afloat and in action. In fact, the cruiser later led the squadron to within 2,200 yards (1,829 meters) of the shore and opened a deadly fire that silenced the last guns at Sangley Point.

INTO CAÑACAO BAY

Shortly after 11 A.M., the seven Spanish warships lay in blazing ruins. The guns at Sangley Point were quiet. Black smoke rolled into the sky from the Cavite base. Dewey, seeing that the battle was all but won, sent the *Concord* and *Petrel* into Cañacao Bay to put an end to any resistance remaining at Cavite and Fort San Felipe. The pair were assigned to the task because both were small and would not run aground in Caña-cao's shallow waters.

As they were passing through the smoke and flame of the Spanish line, the *Petrel*'s captain, Commander Edward Wood, glimpsed a battle flag still flying above one burning ship, the *Don Antonio de Ulloa*. He loosed a few shots in its direction. There was no answering fire. The enemy ship had been abandoned by a crew that had forgotten to lower the flag when they went over the side.

Leaving the *Ulloa* behind, the *Petrel* moved into the navy yard at Cavite. Wood now sighted the masts of moored ships looming behind a line of warehouses.

He began loosing shells into their midst and, several minutes later, saw a white flag rise above the red roofs.

His next stop was off the southern wall of Fort San Felipe. The installation had taken a terrible beating all morning long and was now pummeled by the approaching *Petrel*. The San Felipe's commander, his ammunition exhausted and his men needlessly being sacrificed, put an end to the morning's fighting. A white flag rose above the crumbling fort.

The *Petrel* signaled word of the fort's surrender to Dewey. Immediately, all the American guns fell silent. The time was 1:20 P.M. Eight hours had passed since the Spanish had opened fire at 5:15 that morning. The battle for Manila Bay was at an end.

Chapter 5—Looking Toward Cuba

For the Spanish, the battle was a catastrophe. Admiral Montojo lost ten ships—the seven on the line facing Dewey and three small vessels at the Cavite base. Of his 1,875 men, 167 had been killed and 214 wounded. Wounded himself, he had directed the final moments of the fighting from a convent at Cavite, with his leg torn by a chunk of shrapnel.

On the American side, Dewey had no time to savor his triumph—a mighty victory in trade for a few dents and holes in his ships and only eight minor wounds among his 1,748 men. There was too much else to do in the wake of the fighting.

First, the commodore docked his squadron at Cavite and set about making repairs. Next, he had his men assist in the care of the enemy wounded. Then he sent two ships out to demand the surrender of the troops on Corregidor and other bay islands. Finally, on hearing that the people of Manila feared that the Americans would harm them, he sailed the *Olympia* up to the city and had the ship's band serenade the throngs on shore with Spanish melodies.

Above all else, Dewey set about solving a problem that had bothered him ever since the start of the

Manila campaign. Though he had won the bay, he did not send men ashore to take the city. Some 39,000 enemy troops—divided into 25,000 Spanish soldiers and 14,000 loyalist Filipino fighters—were facing him in the Philippines. Of that number, between 10,000 and 15,000 were based at Manila. He simply did not have the manpower to capture and hold the city.

The Manila plan had always called for army units to join Dewey in taking the city. Those troops were now being mustered in San Francisco under the command of Major General Wesley Merritt and would soon be sailing westward. But they were not expected for weeks. Somehow, during that time, the commodore had to keep the Spanish in check.

To help with the problem, he brought a twenty-nine-year-old Filipino fighter to Manila after months of exile in Hong Kong. His name was Emilio Aguinaldo.

Like Cuba, the Philippines had been rocked by uprisings against the Spanish in the 1890s. Among the revolutionary leaders was Aguinaldo, a man of mixed Tagalog and Chinese blood. He had gone into exile in Hong Kong when the uprisings were quelled in 1896. Now, at Dewey's request, he came to Manila Bay, met with the commodore, and agreed to help the Americans by waging a guerrilla war against the Spanish. He then stole ashore and began to reassemble his fellow revolutionaries for the task. Hordes of men rushed to his side by month's end. They took control of a series of towns on Luzon and other islands. Some 10,000 of their number surrounded Manila and penned in its Spanish troops.

Though Aguinaldo would be of great help to the Americans, he was also destined to be just as great a headache. He had no desire to see them replace the Spanish in the Philippines. His beloved islands were for the Filipinos—and for them alone. He would soon come to hate the Americans as intruders who had to be driven out.

THE FOCUS SHIFTS

While Dewey waited for General Merritt's arrival, the focus of the war shifted back to the United States. There, a totally unprepared army was spending a hectic May trying to ready itself for the fighting.

Like the navy, the army had been reduced in size in the wake of the Civil War. But, unlike the navy, it had not been given the funds to rebuild itself in recent years. Its Regular troops were limited to just over 28,100 officers and men augmented by 100,000 National Guard units in the states. The Regulars were a well-trained and disciplined force, but without the manpower and equipment to engage in a major fight.

At first, however, they were not expected to engage in a major fight, not with the original war plans calling for the navy to blockade Cuba and take Manila Bay. The Cuban blockade was to be handled by the North Atlantic Squadron, commanded by Rear Admiral William Sampson. The government in Washington felt that Sampson's ships and the Cuban revolutionaries together would defeat the Spanish—the ships by choking off help from Spain, and the rebels by making life miserable for the Spanish ashore. Then the army would move in to occupy the island. There would probably never be any direct fighting between the Spanish and the U.S. troops.

With this idea in mind, Major General Nelson Miles, the army's ranking officer, got ready to assemble an occupation force of 80,000 men. They would be trained and equipped for duty at war's end, which would likely come in a matter of months. It was a prudent plan, which called for the steady buildup and training of the force. But it never bore fruit. It was fated to be abandoned soon after war was declared.

THE ARMY: GROWING LIKE A WILD WEED

On the heels of the *Maine* disaster in February, Congress began to increase the strength of the Regular army to give the Miles plan a good start. Next, with the declaration of war in April, there was a boost to 62,000 men. At the same time, President McKinley called for 125,000 volunteers, many of whom would come from National Guard units. Later, Congress approved the addition of more than 35,000 men to the volunteer forces.

These calls proved to be a mistake, but McKinley made them for two reasons. First, the public, egged on by news tycoons Hearst and Pulitzer, was pressuring him for a decisive move in Cuba. Second, now that his efforts to avoid a war had failed, he wanted the swift victory that a mighty army could bring.

Why were the calls a mistake? The army could use 61,000 men for the Miles plan, yes, but not a flood of more than 200,000 volunteers. They were far too many for it to handle. There was sure to be chaos.

And chaos there was. It exploded as soon as word of Dewey's triumph at Manila reached home in May. A tidal wave of patriotism washed across the country, adding to the public fervor already felt for the war. Thousands of men, in the words of the press, began to "flock to the colors."

The result: the army grew like a wild weed in that hectic May. The army's strength would eventually swell to almost 275,000 troops by the time peace returned. There would be 59,000 Regulars and 216,000 volunteers—about ten times the number of men who had been in uniform at the time the war was declared. They added up to far more men than were ever needed for the fighting in both Cuba and the Philippines, and far more than the army could house, feed, arm, and train on what was no more than a moment's notice.

Overnight, countless men began flocking into giant tent camps where they were supposed to be equipped and trained for the Cuban fighting. They

A rustic dining area in the camp in Tampa, Florida

Dewey: The Hero of Manila

The news of the victory at Manila Bay instantly made Commodore Dewey a national hero. Newspapers were packed with stories of his calm leadership in the fighting—and with stories of his immediate promotion to rear admiral by President McKinley, of the $10,000 sword that Congress was having made for him, and of how his men were to be awarded special bronze medals.

A Dewey hysteria swept the country. The sale of American flags vaulted with word of the Manila victory. Manufacturers turned out everything from dishware and drinking glasses to hats, canes, and scarves, all imprinted with Dewey's image. William Randolph Hearst's *New York Evening Journal* staged a fireworks extravaganza in the admiral's honor that was attended by more than 100,000 people.

Dewey songs were heard in vaudeville theaters everywhere. Newspapers and magazines were festooned with poems dedicated to the newly appointed rear admiral, among them the following comic work:

> Oh, dewy was the morning
> Upon the first of May,
> And Dewey was the Admiral,
> Down in Manila Bay.
> And dewy were the Spaniards' eyes,
> Them orbs of black and blue;
> And dew we feel discouraged?
> I dew not think we dew!

Dewey was promoted to the rank of full admiral in early 1899. When he returned home in September of that year, he was given a hero's welcome by New York City. A special arrangement enabled him to remain in the navy beyond retirement age. From 1910 until his death in 1917, he oversaw the formulation of naval strategies for use in the event of war with Germany and Japan.

Admiral Dewey was welcomed to New York with a parade and the presentation of a ceremonial sword— a gift of the nation.

received some training, but for the most part they ran into nothing but confusion. There were no arms, blankets, and tents waiting for them, no lightweight uniforms needed for duty in Cuba's blazing heat. Nor was there any heavy equipment on hand. Everything was hurriedly being thrown together and had yet to arrive.

Waiting instead was food that the men loathed from their first tastes and immediately christened "embalmed beef." And waiting were dangerously inadequate medical and sanitary facilities. They triggered diseases that would take the lives of 2,565 victims.

A NEW PLAN: INVASION

While chaos reigned everywhere, Secretary of War Russell Alger abandoned the army's original plan for the war. He gave in to the ever-mounting public clamor for immediate action in Cuba and set aside the Miles strategy in favor of one of his own. He ordered Miles to muster an army force at points along the nation's southern coast—all within easy reach of Cuba. Once in place, the troops would stand ready to invade Cuba.

At first, Alger intended to send the invaders ashore at Havana. As the seat of the Spanish government in Cuba, the city was a logical choice. But it was also just a tentative one. The selection of a final target had to wait until the whereabouts of a Spanish fleet was determined. The fleet, commanded by Vice Admiral Pascual Cervera and based in the Cape Verde Islands off the west coast of Africa, was known to be sailing to Cuba with fresh troops, arms, and supplies. But all attempts by Sampson's blockading ships to find and intercept the enemy had thus far failed.

No one knew where Cervera would land. Would he choose Havana? Or some other spot on the island? (There were even panicky rumors, all unfounded, that he was heading for some point along the U.S. coastline.) Wherever the Spanish admiral dropped anchor in Cuba, that would become Alger's target.

The U.S. invasion force was to be made up of Regular troops accompanied by several volunteer outfits. One of the volunteer units—a cavalry regiment—was destined to become the most famous fighting group in the war.

THE ROUGH RIDERS

When President McKinley issued his call for 125,000 volunteers, he also authorized the formation of three unique regiments—unique because they would be

"composed exclusively of frontiersmen possessing special qualifications as horsemen and marksmen." When the three took shape, the one that caught the public eye was the 1st United States Volunteer Cavalry or, as it was soon nicknamed by the press, the Rough Riders.

Chiefly responsible for the unit's new fame was its assistant commander, Lieutenant Colonel Theodore Roosevelt. Roosevelt, affectionately known to the public as Teddy (a name he privately

Colonel Theodore Roosevelt in 1898

The Rough Riders

The men of the Rough Riders made their troop into one of the most unusual units ever to serve in the United States Army, this because they came from two widely separated socioeconomic classes.

At one extreme, there were wealthy young college men from the nation's finest universities, among them Harvard, Princeton and Columbia—men such as Hamilton Fish, the grandson of President Ulysses S. Grant's secretary of state. At the opposite extreme, there were cowboys, Indian fighters, and lawmen from the far West, rugged men represented by the likes of Benjamin Daniels, who had once been the marshal at Dodge City and who had half an ear chewed off in a fight while serving there.

Though the two groups were as different from each other as they could be, they shared two characteristics in common. First, they were all superb horsemen. Second, as Theodore Roosevelt was to write, they "possessed in common the traits of hardihood and a thirst for adventure. They were to a man born adventurers."

Roosevelt himself was a "born adventurer." Born in 1858, he was a frail youngster who grew into an

detested), was not only the energetic assistant secretary of the navy but also a recognized athlete, rancher, and hunter, plus both a good horseman and marksman. Secretary of War Alger so admired these qualities that he considered Roosevelt to be the perfect choice to lead the new regiment and offered him its command.

Roosevelt refused the offer, saying that he was too inexperienced in "military work" for the job. He did, however, agree to accept the post of assistant commander and successfully urged that a veteran officer, Colonel Leonard Wood, be appointed commander.

Some two thousand men from all walks of life hurried to enlist in the outfit at its camp outside of San enthusiastic outdoorsman and horseman, traveling widely in the West and, at one time, spending two years as a rancher in Dakota Territory. In the 1880s he started on the way to winning fame as a writer and politician. As a writer, he produced biographies of two well-known early American political figures (Senators Gouverneur Morris and Thomas Hart Benton) and a four-volume history titled *The Winning of the West*. He began his political career as a member of the New York Assembly, won the state's governorship, became vice president under William McKinley in the election of 1900, entered the White House as the nation's 26th president in 1901 following McKinley's assassination, and then earned the post for himself in the 1904 election. Much credit for his winning of the presidency belonged to his service with the Rough Riders. The unit became the most famous outfit to serve in Cuba.

Leonard Wood, who was assigned to the command of the Rough Riders, could boast an unusual "twist" to his military career. He entered the army as a physician after earning his medical degree at Harvard in 1884. However, he eventually won fame not as a medical officer but as regular officer, rising to the rank of major general in 1903, serving as the military governor of Cuba at war's end, and going on to become the army's chief of staff from 1910 to 1914.

Antonio, Texas. There, they would be close to the Gulf of Mexico when the time came for the Cuban invasion. Roosevelt joined them in mid-May after completing the last of his Navy Department duties.

CERVERA DISCOVERED

For the first three weeks in May, the navy kept a frustrated eye out for the elusive Admiral Cervera. Sampson's blockading ships searched all along the island's coast—to no avail. Throughout the hunt, General Miles prepared for the army invasion, saying that if

Cervera was not sighted soon, he would put his troops ashore at Havana.

In the end, Cervera slipped through the U.S. net and, on May 19, landed at Cuba—not at Havana but far away at the port city of Santiago de Cuba on the island's southern coast. It was there that Sampson finally found the enemy admiral and his fleet of four cruisers, two destroyers, and several small support vessels. The long search was over.

Hovering 5,000 yards (4,572 meters) offshore, Sampson swung his guns toward the harbor and opened fire.

Chapter 6—Striking at Cuba

Santiago de Cuba lies on an oblong bay, 6 miles (10 kilometers) long and 3 miles (5 kilometers) wide, about 6 miles inland from the Caribbean. The bay is entered via a narrow, winding channel. Rocky walls, towering as high as 200 feet (60 meters), loomed above the waterway, with army installations dotting their crests. Three forts guarded the heights above the channel entrance—two on the east side and one on the west.

Sampson opened the fighting by bombarding the three forts, after which he intended to sail along the channel, defeat Cervera, and take the city. But he abandoned the plan when his shells failed to silence the forts. Knowing that the channel was mined, he dared not try to inch past the hidden dangers while enemy guns blasted him from above.

He decided that he must first trap his Spanish foe in the bay by blocking the channel. Then he would send for army troops to take Santiago. And so, off to the War Department went a request for army help, and into the channel went a small collier, the *Merrimac*. Its skipper was under orders to turn the ship broadside in the channel and sink it.

The maneuver failed. When the *Merrimac* went down, it blocked only a portion of the channel width. There was just enough room for Cervera to slip past and dash to the sea. The *Merrimac*'s action was an exceedingly dangerous one. As a consequence, though the attack was a failure, the American crewmen were all later awarded the Medal of Honor.

Sampson, now facing a long siege while awaiting the army's arrival, sailed a battalion of just over 600 marines (the marines traveled on warships and were part of the U.S. Navy at that time) 50 miles (80 kilometers) eastward to another body of water—Guantánamo Bay. They were to take the bay and establish a base there to serve as a coaling station for his blockading ships and the transports that would bring the army to his side.

The marines were destined to wage the first U.S. land battle on Cuban soil. It was a four-day skirmish that began soon after they entered the bay on a steamy June 10 and went ashore to establish a camp on a small hill above the beach. They landed unopposed, but were hit by a Spanish force as they were making camp. The enemy, 300 strong, came charging out of the jungle from a post several miles inland. Two marines and a naval surgeon died in the first moment of the onslaught.

The leathernecks drove the attackers off. Then, joined by 50 Cuban rebels who suddenly materialized on the beach, they stormed inland and took the enemy's main post in the area. The fighting ended in mid-June, with the bay in U.S. hands.

As soon as the War Department received word that Sampson had found Cervera, a stream of orders went out to the troops stationed along the U.S. coast facing Cuba. A force of some 25,000 began to gather at the small Florida resort town of Tampa. There, forming

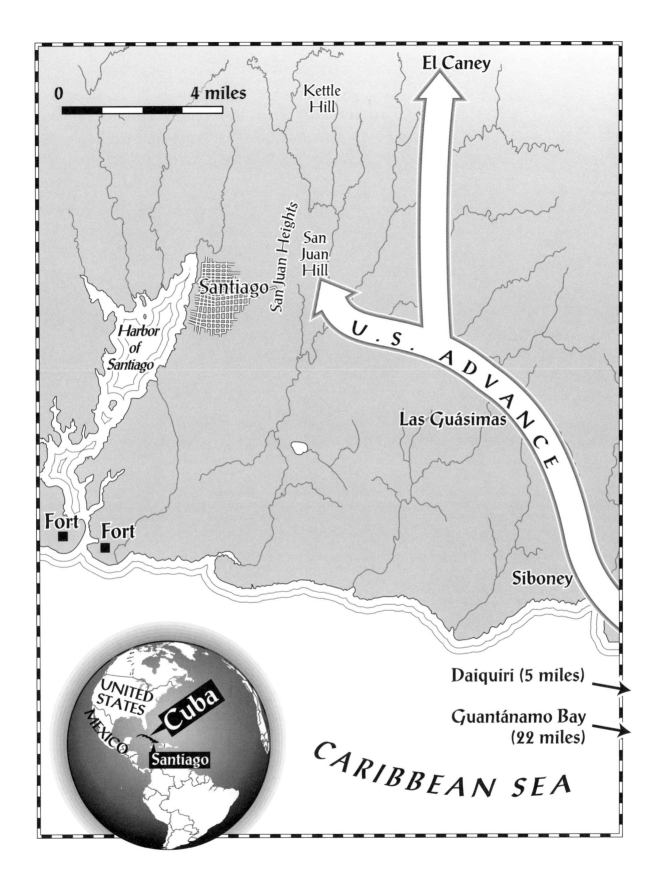

El Caney

Kettle
Hill

0   4 miles

San Juan
Hill

San Juan Heights

Santiago

Harbor
of
Santiago

U. S. ADVANCE

Las Guásimas

Fort   Fort

Siboney

Daiquiri (5 miles) →

Guantánamo Bay
(22 miles) →

CARIBBEAN SEA

UNITED
STATES

Cuba

MEXICO

Santiago

the 5th Army Corps, they would board transports and then sail to Santiago and join with the navy for an attack on the city.

In command of the 5th Corps was aging, 300-pound (136-kilogram) Major General William Shafter, who had been gathering a force at Tampa as part of the Miles invasion plan. There was no camp at Tampa but just a flat, dusty plain surrounding the town and crowded with newly pitched tents. Now, on May 31, came the order to prepare for a host of incoming troops and the voyage to Santiago.

General Shafter, very heavy and suffering from gout, rides through Cuba evaluating the situation.

THE HECTIC WEEKS

The order marked the opening of two hectic weeks. Several factors were responsible, chief among them the choice of Tampa as the invasion's launching point. The little resort town had only one advantage for the army: It was especially close to Cuba. Otherwise, it had little to offer—only small Port Tampa located 9 miles away (15 kilometers) and boasting just a single pier for loading ships and one single track railroad coming in from the outside; once a train reached the port, it could only leave by backing out. The port simply could not handle all the arriving troops, their gear, and the crated supplies being shipped in from distant arsenals and factories. A monstrous traffic jam was created. Troop and supply trains were backed up for miles, some as far as Charleston, South Carolina.

Adding to the mess were those crated supplies. Dumped at trackside, they fast became mountains of mystery—mysterious because they had been shipped so quickly that their contents were unmarked. Soldiers spent their days prying them open to determine what was in them. They would spend more days at that job after landing in Cuba. The problem would constantly hamper the U.S. advance to victory.

Adding further to the nightmare was General Shafter's method of command. He was a seasoned frontier fighter, but he had spent his career with small units. He had no experience in handling large-scale operations, and it showed when the troops came pouring in on him. He told their commanders that they—and not his staff—were responsible for getting their men aboard the transports at Port Tampa.

He hoped this strategy would save the time that would be lost in developing a detailed plan for boarding. But it only led to chaos, especially when the troops learned that there were not enough transports for all the units. Some men would be left behind. With everyone determined not to miss out on the coming glorious adventure, there was a daily mad rush to secure a place aboard the transports as, one by one, they came lumbering up to Port Tampa's single pier.

Caught in the melee were Theodore Roosevelt and his Rough Riders. They hurried to Tampa from their base at San Antonio and made camp several miles outside town. On June 7, already angry over being ordered to leave behind their horses (except those owned by the officers) in the name of saving shipboard space, they learned that the invasion fleet was to embark the next morning and that there was no transport to get them to Port Tampa in time for the departure. They faced the tragedy of being left behind.

Well, that wasn't going to happen! Colonel Wood and Roosevelt spent most of the night marching their troops toward Port Tampa. Then, at 3:00 A.M., when still several miles from their destination, they flagged down a train of empty coal cars returning from the port. While the troops happily clambered aboard, the two officers talked the engineer into backing the train all the way to the port's dockside.

Covered with coal dust, they faced a final problem on their arrival. They had to find the ship that had been assigned to them. It was the steamer *Yucatán*, which had also been allotted to two other units. Roosevelt and Wood watched the surrounding troops grab any ship they could lay their hands on. When the two sighted the *Yucatán* approaching dockside, they seized an unused launch and sped out to the ship. Wood then had the captain guide the ship to a landing, while Roosevelt dashed back to shore and brought a squad of

This lithograph was drawn using eyewitness accounts of the Las Guasimas battle. On the left you can see the Spanish troops hidden in the brush.

Rough Riders to dockside. Hurrying aboard as soon as the *Yucatán* came alongside, the squad stood guard against all comers as Roosevelt fetched the rest of the Riders and rushed them to the steamer.

The invasion force was ready to sail on June 8, but was held from putting to sea until the 14th. Causing the delay was the report that two ships, thought to be Spanish, had been sighted somewhere nearby. Dubbed the "Phantom Fleet," the two were finally identified as U.S. vessels.

SAILING TO CUBA

Sailing aboard 32 transports were not the 20,000 men originally scheduled for the invasion but about 17,000—819 officers and slightly more than 16,000 men. They were divided among 40 units that made up:

Two infantry divisions—the 1st and 2nd—consisting of 18 Regular and two volunteer regiments.

A dismounted cavalry division (called dismounted because the troopers left their horses behind and fought on foot) consisting of 10 Regular and two voluntary outfits.

One cavalry troop, mounted.

Six artillery batteries.

One Gatling Gun (machine gun) company.

One balloon detachment for battlefield observation.

Making up a major percentage of the force were Regular army troops. Among them were two crack African-American units—the 9th and 10th Cavalry regiments. Volunteers accounted for only 2,465 men.

Escorted by warships, the transports made their way through a tranquil sea under blazing skies to a meeting with Sampson's fleet off the Santiago coast on June 20. Shafter and the admiral met and stole ashore for a secret conference with General Calixto García, the commander of all rebel troops in eastern Cuba.

Seated in a jungle hut, the three men developed a plan for taking Santiago. Sampson urged Shafter to order his troops to scale the walls to either side of the channel entrance for an attack on the forts atop them. After Shafter had driven the Spanish from their guns, Sampson would clear the channel of its mines, sail into the bay, and attack Cervera.

Shafter refused to have his troops climb to forts atop 220-foot (67-meter)-high cliffs. Exposed to enemy fire from above, they would be committing suicide. Instead, he accepted a suggestion from García—that he land at the coastal village of Daiquiri about 16 miles (26 kilometers) east of Santiago and then thrust overland to the city.

García admitted that a landing at Daiquiri could be dangerous. The village, a collection of thatched huts, stood on a broad beach that lay in the shadow of high bluffs. The bluffs and a blockhouse atop their highest peak were manned by 300 Spanish soldiers so well entrenched that they could annihilate a massive landing force. But the general promised that his rebels could take care of this threat. They would hit the defenders from behind and drive them off.

And so Shafter decided to go ashore at Daiquiri. He would then move west for an attack on San Juan Heights, a complex of hills about 2 miles (3 kilometers) outside Santiago. Once past them, he would have a clear run to Santiago.

Facing Shafter would be the commander of Spain's 4th Army Corps, General Arsenio Linares. Some 36,000 soldiers were serving under him in the area around Santiago. Of that number, 12,000 were on duty in the city itself, with another 5,000 stationed between the city and Daiquiri.

THE LANDING AT DAIQUIRI

Preparations for the landing at Daiquiri began at 4:30 on the morning of June 22, 1898, when the blue-uniformed troops of the 8th Infantry Regiment climbed down accommodation ladders from the transports.

They were to spearhead the landing, and waiting for them at the bottom of the ladders were three armed tugs, a dozen steam launches, and 40 longboats. The troops settled into the longboats, which were roped in strings to the motor launches and were to be towed to the shore.

The loading required several hours, and it was not until well after dawn that the 8th Infantry began to move toward shore, with the longboats plowing through the water behind the steam launches. Up ahead, the men could see the ramshackle huts of Daiquiri and the high iron dock that stood at the water's edge; the dock and several nearby workshops had been built by an American company for shipping Cuban tin out to the world. In front of the dock was a low wooden pier that extended 40 feet (12 meters) out into the water. It was to be the spot where the first troops landed.

As the longboats bounced through the surf, Sampson's warships opened fire on the bluffs behind the beach. The incoming shells tore up great chunks of earth and ripped trees out by their roots. But there was something puzzling about those heights and the blockhouse that crowned them. There were enemy gun emplacements up there. Yet there were no cannon flashes to be seen anywhere. The Spanish soldiers were not returning Sampson's fire.

Suddenly, the Americans saw a group of horsemen gallop out of the trees and onto the beach, a Cuban flag flowing above their heads. Then a man ran out on the high iron dock and began to wave a white flag, the prearranged signal that the Spanish defenders had abandoned Daiquiri, obviously ordered by General Linares to take up defensive positions on the road to Santiago. At the sight of the white flag, Sampson

Animals in Distress

Adding to the problems of the Daiquiri landing was the manner of unloading the horses and mules that were permitted to accompany the invasion. Since there was no way of transferring them from the ships to the invasion boats, their handlers had no choice but to herd them to the rails and then push them overboard for a swim to the shore.

Some, confused and frightened, began to swim blindly out to sea. On the beach, regimental buglers saw a tragedy in the making. They immediately began to blow a series of calls familiar to the animals—"Boots and Saddles," "Stables," and even "Charge." Some of the swimmers automatically responded to the brassy notes, swung about, and struggled toward the shore.

Though the buglers prevented the tragic loss of dozens of animals, they could not save the lives of five mounts. One of the five drowned was Rain-in-the-Face, a favorite of Theodore Roosevelt. Roosevelt had managed to bring two horses to Cuba with him, and the second, Little Texas, made its way safely to the beach and served him throughout the Cuban campaign.

halted the bombardment, and the men in the fast-approaching longboats began to cheer. Then, as they clamored up onto the low wooden pier to be greeted with hugs by grinning Cuban rebels, their cheers were picked up by the entire invasion force—all its transports, warships, and auxiliary vessels—and sent echoing far out to sea.

The landing at Daiquiri was made against no opposition whatsoever. The Spanish flag above the blockhouse was soon brought down by members of the Rough Riders. An American flag rose in its place and triggered more cheers throughout the invasion fleet.

Though unopposed, the landing, however, was not free of problems. Much trouble was caused by the captains of the troop transports. The transports were supposed to follow the spearheading 8th Infantry up to the shore and disgorge their troops and equipment on the iron pier. But because they were privately owned vessels that had been leased by the government, their captains had the right to protect them from being harmed. Fearing that the vessels would run aground, many of the skippers refused to sail up to the pier. Instead, they crowded their troops into ships' boats offshore and let them get to the beach as best they could, a precaution that delayed the troop arrivals for hours and led to assorted mishaps. Some boats capsized in the surf, dumping their men into the water. Others sank when they were overloaded with artillery pieces, ammunition, and food supplies.

Despite all the problems and confusion, the Americans had 6,000 men ashore by nightfall of June 22, with 11,000 more to follow in the next two days. Of that number, only two men lost their lives when the boat in which they were riding capsized in the surf. Both were seasoned Regulars with a black infantry unit.

Now the invaders faced the march on Santiago and the land and sea battles that would bring the war in Cuba to a victorious end for the Americans and the Cuban rebels.

Chapter 7—Four Hills to Santiago

While sailing to Cuba, the Americans had thought that their only enemies would be the Spanish. Their first night ashore, and then the march toward Santiago, proved them completely wrong.

On camping along the beach at Daiquiri, they came under attack by new adversaries—countless giant land crabs. The creatures suddenly appeared everywhere and began crawling into the two-man tents. The darkness soon echoed with the angry curses of sleepers who awoke to find the things clinging to their hair, ears, and noses.

The next days brought another enemy—the trails that led west to Santiago. They were narrow, with barely enough room for the men to march two abreast. Further, they poked their way through jungle growth so thick that scouts could not venture out to either side to warn of snipers or enemy troops preparing to attack.

Still further, the trails were unpaved. The rainy season had arrived while the Americans were still sailing to Cuba. Now, heavy downpours daily turned the paths into brownish streams. The troops slogged along up to their ankles in sticky mud.

The worst of the enemies was the hot, humid weather. The men, wearing woolen uniforms, lived and fought in rain- and sweat-soaked clothing. The voyage to Cuba in the sweltering heat had already weakened them, and now the humidity drained the rest of their strength away. They dropped as they marched and had to be hospitalized.

The move westward began at the end of the first day's action. General Shafter, watching from his flagship, saw that Daiquiri was an impossible spot for the landing of supplies. He ordered the troops already ashore to shift westward for 7 miles (11 kilometers) to the coastal village of Siboney. It promised far better landing conditions.

Though forced to battle a narrow and muddy trail, most of the men were settled in Siboney within two days. Once there, they received new orders from Shafter. They were to wait while the remainder of their comrades and all of their supplies came ashore (the wait promised to be a long one, thanks to the problem of identifying the contents of all those unmarked crates). Only when well equipped would the troops start for Santiago, now 10 miles (16 kilometers) away. Ahead of them loomed four defended hills that had to be surmounted.

HILL #1: THE FIGHT FOR LAS GUÁSIMAS

Shafter's plan called for his two infantry divisions—the 1st and 2nd—to lead the way to the city. Bringing up the rear would be a dismounted cavalry division (dismounted, remember, because only its officers had been allowed to bring their horses to Cuba). A mixture of Regular and volunteer units, it included the 9th and 10th Regular African-American regiments, several white Regular outfits, and the Rough Riders. Heading the division was a former Confederate officer in the Civil War and now an Alabama representative in the United States Congress—Major General Joseph Wheeler.

Wheeler was a small, fiery man whose courage had earned him the nickname "Fighting Joe" in the Civil War. He hated the idea of bringing up the rear in the coming action. He wanted his cavalrymen to win the honor of being the first troops to engage the enemy.

On June 23, when he rode out a short distance along the trail that ran from Siboney to Santiago, Wheeler saw the chance for them to do just that. He stopped to survey a hill called Las Guásimas. It loomed directly in his path, with a line of enemy rifle pits and stone breastworks running along its crest. They spread away from both sides of a small red-roofed adobe farmhouse with riflemen at the windows. Wheeler correctly estimated that the defenders numbered some 2,000. They had to be dislodged if the trail to Santiago was to be cleared—and his men were the perfect ones for the job.

But what of Shafter's orders to bring up the rear? Shafter had written those orders while aboard his flagship. He was still out at sea, crippled with gout in one leg and saddled with the job of landing his army's mystery crates. Wheeler, as the ranking officer ashore, decided to drive the Spanish from Las Guásimas immediately, before they grew any stronger.

And so, without informing Shafter, he sent his troops against the hilltop on June 24. At dawn, with Colonel Wood and Theodore Roosevelt in the lead, the Rough Riders started hiking up a narrow track from Siboney. About a mile off to their right, two dismounted regiments—the 1st and 10th—made their way along a wagon road that joined the track at the Spanish defense line. With heavy foliage choking the land all around, the units were unable to spread out in an attack formation. They had to stick to the trails, where they became much easier targets for the enemy fire.

The first rattle of that fire erupted at about 7:30 A.M. The opening shots were wild. Some fell short of their mark, others went wide, and still others whistled overhead through the treetops. Roosevelt later wrote that the overhead shots sounded like "the humming of telegraph wires." But soon the Spanish rifles began to find their targets. Here and there along the line of march, Rough Riders began to fall.

Roosevelt was deeply impressed by the way his men reacted when hit. They did not cry out in pain. They fell in silence, with some saying only, "I got it that time." Roosevelt was also impressed with Wood's calm behavior; it soothed the men and won the colonel the nickname "Old Icebox." When the Riders were once pinned down by the enemy fire, Wood heard some men cursing. He strode along the trail repeating the quiet order, "Don't swear—shoot!"

And shoot they did. Their opening shots were like those of the Spanish—wild and wide of their marks. But they soon found their targets, striking the first as they were beginning to climb toward the red-roofed farmhouse that anchored the Spanish line.

At about the same time, to Roosevelt's right, the men of the 1st and 10th caught sight of the enemy trenches spreading away to either side of the farmhouse. They wheeled two cannons to the head of the line and, as best they could, spread out into the tall grass and undergrowth to either side of the trail. When the cannons opened fire, the troopers moved upward, struggling over lines of barbed wire that had been strung across their path and ducking low to avoid the rifle fire that broke above their heads.

Over on his trail, Roosevelt heard the roar of the cannons and, minutes later, the sound of cheering. That cheering had to mean just one thing: the 1st and 10th had reached the hilltop and were driving the Spanish off. He acted in an instant. Shouting for his men to follow him, he hiked to the summit. There, on reaching the small farmhouse, he found the place abandoned. Littering the floor beneath the windows and in the doorway were piles of empty shell casings.

Just before the troops left to fight for Las Guásimas, the three journalists on the left (in civilian clothes) finished their breakfast. One of the three worked for the Hearst New York Journal, *and was badly wounded as he covered the attack.*

The fighting for Las Guásimas had lasted just two hours, fought by a rearguard unit that had held off the Americans for as long as possible before withdrawing to positions closer to Santiago. The struggle to clear the hilltop had cost Wheeler 52 men wounded and 16 killed. Of that number, the Rough Riders lost 38 men wounded and 8 killed.

When compared with other battles, the fight for Las Guásimas, though courageous, was no more than a skirmish. But, thanks to the newspaper correspondents who accompanied the troops, it was reported as a major battle and a great victory. The reports filled the people back home with pride, which was to grow when Las Guásimas was followed by an even greater triumph—the assault on three hills that were the last obstacles looming between the Americans and Santiago.

HILL #2: THE FIGHTING AT EL CANEY

General Shafter, though angered by the Las Guásimas attack, did not take disciplinary action against the fiery Wheeler. Rather, he rested the troops for several days, nursed his gouty leg, and watched his supplies continue to struggle ashore before attempting the next step in the Santiago campaign.

It was to be an attack against three hills. Two were located in what were called the San Juan Heights about 2 miles (3 kilometers) outside Santiago. The third rose near the tiny village of El Caney, some 3 miles (5 kilometers) to the north of the Heights. Starting in the south, the trio would be hit by the 1st Infantry Division, next by Wheeler's cavalry, and then by the 2nd Infantry Division. In all, some 14,000 Americans would take part in the action.

Assisting them would be a contingent of Cuban fighters under General Gracie. They would station themselves behind the Spanish lines to cut off any troops that came marching out from Santiago to help defend the Heights.

The attack began at dawn on July 1. The 1st Infantry Division and Wheeler's cavalry moved slowly toward the base of San Juan Heights. To Wheeler's north, the 2nd Infantry hit the village of El Caney. Led by Brigadier General Henry Lawton, the 2nd Infantry was to capture the village and cut off the threat of enemy help coming through it from farther north. Once El Caney fell, Lawton was to rush south to join the battle for the Heights.

General Shafter knew that El Caney was defended by a mere 500 men because the Spanish commander, General Linares, had moved the bulk of his troops to defensive positions closer to Santiago. The El Caney defenders were without artillery and machine guns, and were outnumbered ten to one by Lawton's 5,400-man division. Shafter estimated that the village would be taken in just two hours.

He was dead wrong. Armed only with rifles, the Spanish pinned down the Americans all morning long. Their defense was most stubborn atop a low hill south of the village. Like Las Guásimas, it was topped with a small stone building—this time, a fort—surrounded by rifle pits. Lawton first tried to reduce the fort with a battery of four 3.2-inch (81-millimeter) guns, and failed because it was out of their range.

When the artillery proved useless, Lawton hurled two infantry attacks at the little place. He spent the first assault watching a merciless enemy fire cut his

The charge up San Juan Hill

men down as they charged uphill through tall grass. At mid-morning, he called the action off and rested the troops for three hours in preparation for the second attack. During those hours, an infuriating message arrived from Shafter. Unnerved by the splendid enemy defense, Shafter wanted Lawton to break away from El Caney and move south to help at San Juan Heights. Lawton flatly refused. His men were too deeply committed to the El Caney fight to give up.

His second attack began in the early afternoon and took the Americans up to within 150 yards (137 meters) of the fort. Lawton then sent for the deadliest of his riflemen—his marksmen and sharpshooters. They were to come forward and be the only ones now to take aim at the enemy. About 40 of their number crept to the front of the line and opened fire. Everywhere on the hilltop, as he had expected, figures began to lurch and fall—in the rifle pits and in the doorways and gun ports of the fort itself.

The deadly fire soon won the day for the 2nd Infantry. The Americans saw the toppling figures and then watched other figures climb out of the rifle pits and flee west. The Americans sprang to their feet and dashed to the hilltop. The fort was theirs, as were the rest of El Caney's defenses by late afternoon.

The magnificent Spanish defense at El Caney had lasted 10 hours and had kept the 2nd Infantry from joining the main assault on San Juan Heights. Of the 500 Spanish defenders, 420 lost their lives or were wounded. The fighting cost Lawton 360 men wounded and 81 dead.

HILLS #3 AND #4: SAN JUAN HEIGHTS

While Lawton fought at El Caney, the 1st Division and Wheeler's cavalry started toward San Juan and Kettle Hills, the two principal hills in the San Juan Heights. Together, again because the Spanish commander, Linares, had moved the bulk of his troops closer to Santiago, the two hills were defended by an estimated 500 men.

Up against approximately 10,000 Americans, the 500 troops were more outnumbered than their comrades at El Caney. Yet from the beginning of the action, they proved to be implacable foes.

The Americans opened the day by bringing four 3.2-inch (81-millimeter) guns to bear on the enemy. The smoke produced by their firing, however, pinpointed their positions for two Spanish cannons up on the Heights. It took less than an hour for the pair to silence the American artillery.

During the artillery duel, the U.S. troops began to march along the narrow trails leading to the Heights. A hopelessly snarled traffic jam resulted as men and equipment from a variety of outfits became entangled. Spanish rifles—and then artillery when the battle with the American cannons ended—poured a rain of steel death down on the trails. One U.S. trooper later wrote that the ground underfoot became slippery not with mud but with the blood of the wounded and dead.

At one point, the trails crossed a shallow stream. Here, an observation balloon was raised above the trees to give two young Signal Corps officers a look at the defenses ahead. Instantly, it became a prime target for the enemy rifles. Within minutes, it was riddled with bullets and sinking slowly into the trees.

The Spanish gunners, knowing that the balloon pinpointed the vanguard of the U.S. advance, concentrated their fire on the spot, inflicting losses so heavy that the men of one volunteer outfit fled the scene. A unit of African-Americans from the 10th Cavalry rushed forward to take their places. The cavalrymen were led by a young captain who would win world fame twenty years later when, as General John J. Pershing, he would command the U.S. forces in World War I.

Roosevelt and some 50 Rough Riders followed Pershing past the frightened volunteers (the future president was now in sole charge of the Riders because Wood had been promoted and had gone to another

unit to replace its ill commander). Riding his beloved horse Little Texas, Roosevelt found himself in a grassy area at the base of Kettle Hill. Clustered all around his Riders were not only Pershing's men but also those from several other regiments. When, at 1:00 P.M., the order came through from headquarters to attack, he galloped Little Texas across the front of the troops, yelling for them to follow him forward. Then off he went charging uphill. He reined in at a wire fence just below the summit, dismounted, and continued on foot. He heard his troops panting behind him. Up ahead, two Spanish defenders suddenly stood and fired at the oncomers. Roosevelt returned the fire with a pistol, missing one but felling the other.

Moments later, the Americans held Kettle Hill. Roosevelt turned toward San Juan Hill in the near distance. While getting his breath back, he watched the men of the 1st Division struggle toward its base, moving across a grassy field like the one below him. Meeting them was a withering enemy fire. Roosevelt

~81~

ordered his mixture of cavalrymen and infantrymen to open fire on the Spanish lines. Then, seeing that the 1st needed more help, he sprang to his feet and charged downward to join the attack. Moments later, he realized that his men were still crouched up at the summit. Not realizing that he failed to give them the order to attack, he tramped back uphill in a fury and unfairly accused them of cowardice. Moments later, he had them at the side of the 1st.

As Roosevelt had watched from Kettle Hill, the men of the 2nd had been totally exposed in the open field and had been in danger of being wiped out by the few Spanish riflemen in a small blockhouse at the summit. The Americans were saved when three Gatling guns came rushing to the front just before Roosevelt's arrival. The trio opened a clattering fire on the blockhouse. They poured 3,600 rounds a minute into the building, uprooted its troops in just nine minutes, and sent them scrambling toward Santiago's outer defenses while the Americans stormed the summit.

The last of the four hills on the road to Santiago had been surmounted. What remained now was the task of taking Santiago itself. The city, however, was to be won in a battle in which the army would not participate.

Chapter 8—Everywhere, Victories

General Shafter spent July 2 and 3 moving his troops past San Juan Heights to form a curving line along Santiago's eastern side, about a mile from the city limits. But as they moved into place, they had no feeling of being conquerors. Facing them were heavy Spanish defenses, which battered them with artillery and rifle fire and exacted a heavy toll in casualties.

An alarmed Shafter counted his losses. In the three days since moving against the Heights, he had lost 1,180 men wounded and 205 killed while the Spanish had lost just a fraction of their troops in the area—215 killed and 376 wounded. Now, on July 3, facing the loss of even more men, he cabled Secretary of War Russell Alger to say that he was thinking of moving 5 miles (8 kilometers) to the rear so that his troops would be less exposed to the enemy fire.

The message shook Alger. The press was headlining the taking of the Heights as a mighty victory. In the minds of Americans everywhere, that victory would instantly be turned into a defeat if Shafter suddenly seemed to retreat. Alger advised him to stay where he was.

The desperate Shafter next appealed to Admiral Sampson, urging him to sail up the channel to Santiago Bay and take the city. In so doing, the admiral would save hundreds of army lives. Sampson shook his head. He knew he would achieve nothing but the loss of his ships if he dared to challenge the mined and heavily fortified channel.

Shafter had nowhere left to turn for help. But help did arrive. It came from a totally unexpected source, Spanish Admiral Pasqual Cervera. And it came on the very day that Shafter sent his telegram to Secretary Alger—July 3.

CERVERA'S DASH FOR FREEDOM

Ever since the invasion, life had been intolerable for the civilians and military personnel at Santiago. Sampson's fleet had cut them off from all help from the sea, while Shafter's troops had severed their water supply from El Caney and had interfered with the shipment of food from the interior.

Weak with hunger, the Spanish knew that they could neither long defend the city nor launch a successful counterattack against the Americans. It was only a matter of time before thirst and starvation brought Santiago to its knees.

Consequently, Cervera was ordered to bolt for freedom, sail to Cienfuegos on Cuba's northwest coast, and continue fighting for as long as possible. Cervera accepted the order without a word. He knew he faced certain defeat at U.S. hands. His four cruisers and two destroyers—all lightly armed—would be no match for the waiting U.S. fleet.

On the morning of July 3, seven U.S. ships were guarding the entrance to the channel—the battleships *Iowa*, *Indiana*, *Oregon*, and *Texas*, the cruiser *Brooklyn*, and the armed yachts *Gloucester* and *Vixen*. They were under the command of Commodore Winfield Scott Schley because Admiral Sampson was sailing to Siboney for a conference with General Shafter. With Sampson was the cruiser *New York*.

At 9:35 A.M., a surprised Schley saw the Spanish fleet begin to emerge from the channel. First to appear was Cervera's flagship, *Maria Teresa*. Then came its fellow cruisers *Vizcaya*, *Cristóbal Colón*, and *Oquendo*, and the destroyers *Pluton* and *Furor*. They appeared at ten-minute intervals because each had to move cautiously past the *Merrimac*, the collier that had gone aground in the U.S. effort to block the channel.

The *Iowa* opened fire on the *Maria Teresa*. Shells began to rip the Spanish ship apart, littering its deck with dead and wounded crewmen. Cervera swung away from the fire and sighted the *Brooklyn* nearby. Instantly, he saw what must be done. He raced toward the American ship, planning to knock it out of the fighting and open a doorway through which his fleet could slip to the safety of the open sea.

The plan failed just as quickly as it was made. For the next minutes, while the rest of the Spanish fleet was still slipping out of the channel, the *Maria Teresa* absorbed the combined fire of the U.S. ships. All but two of its guns were silenced. Flames erupted everywhere along its decks. Cervera ordered his ship beached.

Soon, the *Maria Teresa* had company. Forced ashore nearby was the *Oquendo*. Both lay burning, with white flags of surrender flying from their masts.

Luckier—at least for a time—were the *Vizcaya* and *Cristóbal Colón*. The air was thick with the smoke of battle when they cleared the channel, and they used it to screen themselves as they sped westward. They were soon sighted, however, with the *Oregon*, *Texas*, and *Brooklyn* giving chase. It was a chase that was to last until early afternoon.

While pursuing the two Spaniards, the *Texas* and *Oregon* hurled some of their shells back toward the channel entrance, where the destroyers *Pluton* and *Furor* were now breaking into the open. Those shells joined the fire from the *Iowa*, *Indiana*, and *Gloucester*. Sampson's flagship, the *New York*, would soon appear on the scene. Sampson had heard the roar of the guns as he was nearing Siboney and had immediately swung about and rushed westward.

The *Gloucester* broke away from its fellow ships and dashed toward the two destroyers. With all guns firing, the American ship forced the *Pluton* aground on the rocky coast, there to die in a blinding explosion. Moments later, a shell from the *Iowa* cut the *Furor* almost in half.

To the west, the running battle with the *Vizcaya* and *Cristóbal Colón* continued. The fighting, however, proved to be too much for the *Vizcaya*. Seeing that his ship was battered beyond endurance, its captain turned shoreward. At 11:00 A.M., the *Vizcaya* lay aground and died.

The *Oregon*, *Brooklyn*, and *Texas*—soon to be joined by Sampson's flagship, the *New York*–now concentrated on pursuing the *Cristóbal Colón*, the fastest of the enemy vessels. But the fleeing ship could not outrun the *Oregon*'s 13-inch (330-millimeter) guns that fired shells weighing 1,100 pounds (500 kilograms) each. At 1:00 P.M., the American ship began

The crew of the Gloucester *goes to the rescue of men scrambling to escape the vanquished* Oquendo.

flinging the gargantuan shells at the *Cristóbal Colón* from 5 miles (8 kilometers) away. The sixth of the lot struck just ahead of the *Cristóbal Colón* and flung a huge blue-white geyser over its forward deck.

The *Cristóbal Colón*'s captain realized that the *Oregon* had found his range and that the next shells were certain to be right on target. He immediately abandoned his flight. Moments later, with a grinding roar, the *Cristóbal Colón* lumbered ashore.

The death of the *Cristóbal Colón* brought the fighting to an end. Instantly, the American crews turned from enemies to rescuers. They realized that the battle had been one-sided, that the Spanish crewmen had performed nobly, and that all the men, no matter on which side they had fought, were really fellow seamen. Ships' boats went quickly into the water and made their way to the grounded Spanish ships, plucking sailors from the water as they went. On shore, the Spaniards greeted their rescuers with open arms; they had been afraid that they would be captured and cruelly treated by Cuban revolutionaries. Their fears were justified. Many had to endure the rifle fire of the revolutionaries while swimming ashore.

Of the 2,200 men in Cervera's fleet, 328 had lost their lives and 151 had been wounded. On the American side, one man had been killed and one had been severely wounded.

TWO SURRENDERS

Cervera's defeat ended the fighting in Cuba. The next weeks were to bring two more surrenders—a bloodless one at Santiago and one with little bloodshed on the nearby Spanish island of Puerto Rico.

By coincidence, on the very day that Cervera attempted his dash for freedom, General Shafter made his first contact with the new commander in Santiago, General José Toral, and urged the surrender of the city to avoid further bloodshed. Toral had just replaced General Linares, who had been wounded.

Though the two sides arranged an exchange of prisoners, Toral was barred by Spanish law from surrendering. He could not capitulate for as long as his men had food and ammunition. They had supplies of both, though both were fast dwindling. Further, Spanish honor demanded that they fight on for as long as possible.

Toral knew that his situation was hopeless. No matter Spanish law, the loss of Santiago was at hand. He watched the numbers of Americans around the city grow greater each day. Their strength was clearly seen on July 10 and 11 when the army and navy joined for a prolonged bombardment of the city.

Shafter continued pressing for a surrender throughout the month. General Nelson Miles, the army's senior commander, joined the negotiations when he arrived in Cuba at mid-month with 3,000 troops. Once Santiago fell, he was to invade Puerto Rico.

Toral finally convinced Spain that his position was hopeless and obtained permission to surrender. The two sides prepared and signed a cease-fire agreement that contained ten provisions. In the main, the pact called for the surrender of all Spanish troops in and around Santiago; the surrender of all their arms; and the transportation back to Spain by the United States of all Spanish soldiers who wanted to return home.

The surrender document was signed by both sides on July 16. At 9:00 o'clock the next morning, Shafter and Toral met in an open field outside Santiago. Each

man was accompanied by his chief officers and a cavalry unit. General Joseph Wheeler was present and wrote that "the Spanish troops presented arms, and the Spanish flag which for 382 years had floated over the city was pulled down and furled forever."

With the surrender, General Miles quickly undertook the task that had brought him to Cuba. He and his 3,000 troops departed Guantánamo Bay on July 21 and sailed to nearby Puerto Rico. Landing at Guánica on its southeastern coast on July 25, he marched inland and brought the island under U.S. control in a matter of days.

MANILA: THE LAST CAMPAIGN

Ever since taking Manila Bay, George Dewey (now promoted to rear admiral) had been waiting patiently for the army troops that would join him in capturing the Philippine capital with its 13,000 Spanish troops. Collected by General Wesley Merritt and assembled at San Francisco and several other California cities was a force of some 18,000 volunteers and Regulars. Between late May and the end of July, they sailed to the Philippines in three separate groups.

The first—a force of 2,500 under Brigadier General Thomas Anderson—stopped at Spanish-held Guam on June 20 and took the island without a fight. It would now serve as a U.S. Navy coaling station. Then Anderson sailed on to Manila Bay, docking at Cavite on June 30 and greeting the rest of the troops in July, with General Merritt himself arriving at month's end.

When all his men were ashore, Merritt moved them to positions behind the line that the Filipino revolutionary leader, Emilio Aguinaldo, had established around Manila's land side. Located 1,000 yards (914 meters) away were the Spanish defensive positions.

Next, using the Belgian consul at Manila as their agent, Merritt joined Dewey in the negotiations aimed at the Spanish surrender of the city. The two Americans felt certain that the Spanish commanders would soon capitulate. Surely, they could see how hopeless their situation was, with Dewey's fleet standing off-

A Strange Moment at Guam

The three transports that made up Brigadier General Thomas Anderson's force approached the island of Guam on June 20, 1898. Escorting the trio was the cruiser *Charleston*, commanded by Captain Henry Glass.

On nearing the island's chief harbor, Glass saw that it was guarded by two ancient forts. Though they appeared to be abandoned, the captain ordered one of the *Charleston*'s batteries to fire a few shots at them. He wanted to determine the correct range should they put up a fight and need to be bombarded.

The fort guns did not reply, but a rowboat soon hurried out from shore and shipped oars alongside the *Charleston*. Then up the accommodation ladder came the port captain and a fellow officer. They saluted smartly on reaching the deck, with the port captain then apologetically telling an astonished Glass:

"You will pardon our not immediately replying to your salute, Captain, but we are not accustomed to receiving salutes here and are not supplied with proper guns for returning them." The Spaniard then politely asked what business brought the Americans to Guam.

When Glass replied, it was the Spaniard's turn to be astonished. The troops at Guam had not received any news from their superiors at Manila since April. They were totally unaware of the fact that Spain and the United States were at war.

The tiny Spanish garrison of 56 marines, knowing the defense of the island was useless, surrendered without firing a shot. Glass ended the bloodless conquest by raising the American flag over the harbor, assigning a small occupation force to remain behind, and placing the Spanish troops aboard one of the transports for the rest of the trip to Manila Bay.

shore and ready to fire while Merritt's Americans and Emilio Aguinaldo's 10,000 insurgents were posed for an attack on the land side.

Badly outnumbered, with only 13,000 troops in the city, the Spanish were willing to surrender but only if the United States agreed to two conditions. First, the Americans would have to stage an attack on the city; Spanish honor demanded that the defenders put up the appearance of a fight before quitting the field. Second, the Spanish authorities knew that Aguinaldo and his men were eager to sweep in and sack the city. It was a specter that made Spanish blood run cold. The Americans would have to promise to keep the Filipino rebels out.

Dewey and Merritt, over Aguinaldo's objections, agreed to the two conditions. Then, on the morning of August 13, they launched a combined attack on Manila. While Dewey's ships opened fire offshore, Merritt's troops shifted to the beaches south of Manila and began to move through Aguinaldo's line. The revolutionary leader had reluctantly agreed to withdraw his fighters to the south when the Americans passed through. Though it was a difficult maneuver, all went well—except for a moment of trouble early on.

It came when an American unit accidentally became mixed in with some of Aguinaldo's men. In the confusion that followed, there were bursts of rifle fire that made the Spanish defenders think that the Americans and Filipinos were firing on *them*. The Spanish quickly readied themselves for a rigorous defense that would have ended the easy conquest of the city. Fortunately, Merritt's officers quickly brought the firing to an end, averting what could have been a disaster for the Americans.

Despite this momentary trouble, the attackers advanced quickly into Manila and took possession of the city by early afternoon, having lost just 17 soldiers killed and 105 wounded. The Spanish formally surrendered the capital the next day, August 14. At the time, Dewey and Merritt were unaware of a vital fact. When Dewey had first taken Manila Bay, he had severed the underwater telegraph cable that connected the Philippines with the outside world. Consequently, he and Merritt had yet to hear the news that the final war of the nineteenth century was over. It had ended in a cease-fire agreement signed by the American and Spanish governments on August 12 after weeks of discussion, and the day before the two men had opened fire on Manila.

Chapter 9—After the Fighting

The negotiations leading to the armistice began on July 13, 1898. The armistice then paved the way to a peace conference held in France from October to December and ending with the signing of the Paris Peace Treaty. The pact was then ratified by the U.S. Senate on February 6, 1899. It contained three major points:

First, Spain relinquished its grip on Cuba, with the island becoming an independent nation. The United States laid no claim to the new country because of an amendment that had been attached to the American declaration of war (see "The Teller Amendment" in chapter 2). The amendment pledged that the United States would not keep Cuba for itself once the war was won.

Next, Spain ceded two islands—Puerto Rico in the Caribbean and Guam in the Pacific—to the United States. Both remain American possessions to this day.

Finally, the United States purchased the Philippine Islands from Spain for the sum of $20 million.

As was explained in chapter 2, the United States had spent the late 1800s transforming itself into a world power. The war and the peace treaty completed the change. But it was a change that would saddle the nation with problems for years to come, especially in Cuba, its surrounding area, and the Philippines.

THE CUBAN PROBLEM

Overseeing the island's stability once the Spanish had departed, a U.S. occupation force remained until heading home in 1902 and leaving behind an independent Cuba. The departure astonished the European powers with colonial holdings. To them, the voluntary surrender of a valuable possession was both shortsighted and foolhardy.

Actually, the truth was that Cuba was not left completely free. The United States kept a grip on the island out of the fear that the Cubans were not yet ready to survive on their own. It did so with what was called the Platt Amendment.

Behind the measure was U.S. Secretary of War Elihu Root. In 1900, when the Cubans were writing a constitution for their new country (basing it on the U.S. Constitution), he noted that it contained no provisions for the continuation of Cuban-American relations. Fearing that the omission would lure other powers into attempting an island takeover, he insisted that the provisions had to be included. Until then, America would not remove its occupation force.

Root then wrote the provisions himself and had Senator Orville H. Platt of Connecticut present them for congressional approval in 1901. Named for the senator, they became an amendment that was to define Cuban-American relations for decades to come. It specified that Cuba would:

Make no treaty that would impair its independence;

Keep its debts within its ability to pay them;

Allow the United States to intervene with force should intervention be needed to maintain order anywhere on the island;

Give the United States the right to establish naval bases on the island. (Out of this provision came the lease—still in force today—for the American base at Guantánamo Bay. The lease cannot be broken except by the consent of both nations.)

In effect, by severely limiting Cuba's ability to act for itself, the amendment turned the infant country into a U.S. protectorate. It enraged the Cubans, especially its clause permitting American intervention in the event of island troubles. As they saw things, their giant neighbor could now poke its nose into their affairs on any pretext whatsoever. But to be rid of the occupation force, they stifled their anger and added the measure to their constitution in 1901. A year later, the occupation troops departed.

THE PHILIPPINES PROBLEM

The Philippines problem centered on a question that deeply troubled President McKinley for months: What could the United States honorably do with the islands now that it had defeated Spain?

He felt that he could not justifiably return them to the oppressive rule of Spain, certainly not after granting Cuba its independence. Nor could America simply leave them on their own. Their population—consisting of various native groups, immigrants from the Asian

American Interventions

The United States first exercised its right to intervene in Cuban affairs in 1906. It was then that the island people rebelled after the reelection of their first president, Tomás Estrada Palma.

Palma was an honest man who had the misfortune of being surrounded by corrupt officials. They pocketed public funds and demanded bribes of anyone who hoped to do business with the government. These offenses outraged the Cubans and caused them to lose confidence in the president.

As a result, Palma feared that he would be soundly beaten in his bid for reelection in 1906. So fearful was he that he abandoned his sense of honesty and won the presidency by "stuffing the ballot box"—that is, by padding the voting rolls with the names of nonexistent people and then having his cronies cast their ballots under those names.

When word of his fraud reached the people, they exploded in rebellion. Insurgent troops surrounded the capital at Havana, threatened to overthrow the government, and caused Palma to resign his post. American marines, rushing in from their base at Guantánamo Bay, restored order, with the United States then governing the island until the election of a new president in 1909.

American troops again occupied Cuba in 1912 and still again between 1917 and 1922. The 1912 occupation was caused by a race war that claimed hundreds of island lives. Accounting for the 1917–1922 occupation was a complex of political and economic problems.

Though the Platt Amendment was used in the Cuban occupations, it could not be employed in other American interventions that came in the postwar years. For example,

mainland, and almost a million primitive tribal people—had been kept under Spain's thumb for centuries. Left alone, with scant experience in self-rule, they could well be grabbed by some European nation. Or there could be civil unrest and, eventually, anarchy.

McKinley decided that there was just one way to solve his dilemma: America must keep the islands for a

Theodore Roosevelt used the Monroe Doctrine to avert a threatened invasion of Venezuela by Great Britain, Germany, and Italy in 1902.

They were Venezuela's major investors, and they sent gunboats into its territorial waters when it could not pay the debts owed to them. Roosevelt waved the trio off by warning them that an invasion would be a violation of the Monroe Doctrine, and he would demand action on America's part. He then successfully urged Venezuela to arbitrate a settlement of all its debts.

A number of other South and Central American countries had trouble paying their debts, prompting their creditors to threaten them with the use of force in making collections. America by then was digging the Panama Canal and did not want the work interrupted by trouble in the surrounding region. To protect the canal, marines were stationed in Nicaragua from 1912 to 1933 (with a brief interruption in 1925) and in Haiti from 1914 to 1934. Citing the Monroe Doctrine as justification, the United States took on the job of collecting import fees for the Dominican Republic and distributing them to the island's government and its creditors; when the Dominican government tried to stop this practice in 1916, marines came ashore and marked the beginning of eight years under an American military government.

Though the United States did not attempt to acquire territorial holdings from these efforts, it did earn the anger of the Central and South American people. In the 1930s, to end that anger and unite the western hemisphere in friendship, President Franklin Roosevelt launched his "Good Neighbor Policy," saying that the United States was opposed to the armed intervention in the internal affairs of any country in the Americas.

As part of that policy, the United States abandoned the Platt Amendment in Cuba and soon began withdrawing its troops from Nicaragua, Haiti, and the Dominican Republic.

time and then grant them their freedom when they were finally ready for it. But even this well-intentioned solution troubled him because of the date of Manila's fall. The city and, by extension, the rest of the islands had been won one day after the armistice had been signed. Thus they could not be justifiably claimed as spoils of war.

Again, McKinley saw a problem with just one solution. Since the United States could not claim the islands, it must buy them. That decision led to a long debate in Paris and a final agreement on the purchase and its price—$20 million. There was also the understanding that the Filipinos would eventually be granted their freedom.

Regardless of McKinley's honorable intentions, the purchase soon caused trouble in the Philippines. Behind the upset was the revolutionary leader Emilio Aguinaldo. He had done a superb job in helping the United States defeat Spain, but he cared as little for the Americans as the Spanish. He wanted all foreigners gone, with his islands left to his people.

Aguinaldo, however, had been happy to help Admiral Dewey and General Merritt. He believed that, once Spain was ousted, America would treat the Philippines just as it was going to treat Cuba. They would be set free. And so, his anger boiled over in mid-1898 when he heard rumors that McKinley and many U.S. leaders were changing their minds about liberating the Philippines and were planning to keep the islands.

That change could be seen in two facts. First, in June, the Americans had taken Guam. Then, in July, they had annexed Hawaii with its fine naval base at Pearl Harbor (they had held rights to the base since 1887). These steps left no doubt that they planned to expand their trade with Asia. The Philippines would now serve as a magnificent base for that trade.

To end what he saw as a terrible threat to his homeland, Aguinaldo established an independent government for the Philippines in early August. He named himself its president and appealed to all foreign nations

The Steps to Philippine Independence

True to President McKinley's intent, the United States eventually honored the promise of independence for the Philippines.

Starting at the close of the war, the Filipinos were given increasing powers of self-government. By 1907 they were electing some of the representatives to their legislature. Nine years later, the Philippine islands were made virtually self-governing (although they lost some of this status during the 1920s).

In 1934 the islands were offered their complete independence in ten years. The next year, they became a self-governing commonwealth under President Manuel Queson y Molino. Complete independence, however, was delayed by World War II, when the islands were attacked by the Japanese in 1941, defeated by mid-1942, and occupied by the invader until war's end in 1945.

Complete independence finally become a reality on July 4, 1946.

to recognize Filipino independence. At the same time, he urged recognition by Dewey and Merritt. The two men, not certain of Washington's exact plans for the islands, angered him by ignoring the request while Merritt's troops poured into Manila Bay.

Aguinaldo was further angered when Merritt banned him from the attack on Manila, and again when his revolutionaries, eager to even the score for centuries of Spanish abuse, tried to enter and ransack the fallen city, only to be stopped at gunpoint by Merritt's soldiers.

Under circumstances that have remained unclear ever since, fighting erupted between Aguinaldo's men and the Americans at Manila on February 4, 1899. The outbreak marked the start of the uprising that has gone down in history as the Philippine Insurrection. In just over two years, the United States sent 100,000 troops to the fighting, took Aguinaldo prisoner, and waged a bloody guerrilla war on Luzon and its surrounding islands. There was still fighting, though weakening, on July 4, 1902, when Theodore Roosevelt, the former Rough Rider and now the 26th president of the United States, announced the formal end of the rebellion. (Due to his wartime exploits and his ability to campaign tirelessly, Roosevelt was elected vice president under McKinley in 1900. He moved to the White House when McKinley was assassinated in 1901.)

THE AMERICAN PROBLEM

The Paris Peace Treaty did more than cause trouble in Cuba and the Philippines. It also triggered an angry debate at home when it was put before the Senate for ratification.

While there were many Americans—from political leaders to ordinary citizens—who applauded the pact and the international strength it promised, there were just as many who opposed it, angrily doing so on two main points.

First, they felt that ratification would put the United States in a dangerous position. Long ago, George Washington had warned the nation against becoming caught in foreign "entanglements." They always brought the risk of war. In general, America had followed his advice and had grown mightily through the years. It would be folly to forget his counsel now.

Second, America was ready to free the Cubans, but not the Filipinos because they were widely considered to be ill prepared for the responsibilities that came with independence. The idea that they could not handle their own affairs and had to be guided by a wiser country smacked of a European view that infuriated many Americans. It was the view that a nation with overseas holdings—along with profiting from those holdings—had the duty to protect and better the lot of the poor natives in their care. This meant that the United States was planning to carry, in the words of a famous phrase of the day, "the white man's burden" in the islands. To many, this was sheer arrogance.

Worse, to keep the Philippines would be a violation of the philosophy voiced in America's Declaration of Independence—that a people shall be governed by their own consent.

Taking an opposite point of view, the supporters of annexation stressed the dangers of leaving the islands on their own—the dangers of placing their government in the hands of inexperienced leaders and leaving the country open to a grab by some European power. Further, annexation promised a treasure trove of business profits for U.S. companies. Finally, above all else, it gave the Americans the right to use the Philippines as a naval base.

The supporters of annexation finally won the day for the treaty in the Senate. They did so by stressing the points that the United States planned to award the Filipinos their freedom in the future and that the war would not end until the Paris Peace Treaty was ratified. And so, the sooner that the Senate stopped arguing and signed the pact, the sooner the United States would be able to grant the Philippine islands their independence.

TWO TRIUMPHS

Though the postwar period was a troublesome one for the United States, it was also a time of two American triumphs. One put an end to a feared disease, and the other gave the world an engineering masterpiece.

The end of the fighting did not end the danger of military service in Cuba. Rather, it pitted the troops against four invisible enemies—dysentery, malaria, typhoid, and yellow fever. Especially feared was yellow fever, an infectious disease born of a virus in Africa and other warm climates. It had been a dreaded presence in South, Central, and North America for more than 200 years. In the United States alone, it had attacked more than 500,000 victims in the previous century and had taken the lives of about 90,000 of their number.

As it had during the war, the disease went on striking down hundreds of U.S. soldiers in Cuba and stateside camps when peace returned. So many troops fell ill that some units were rendered incapable of any duty whatsoever. Deeply troubled, the army's surgeon general appointed a commission to study the disease, find its cause, and then wipe it out.

Heading the commission was Major Walter Reed of the Army Medical Corps. He and his team of doctors investigated the disease for months, with their researches at last bringing them to a long-ignored theory as to how it was spread. The theory ran contrary to the traditional view that yellow fever was spread through contact with its victims or their belongings—their clothing, their bedding, their cooking utensils and dishware. Rather, the theory held, it was spread through the bite of a mosquito—the female *Aedes aegyptia* (or, as it was then known, the *Stegomyia fasciata*).

Reed's doctors put the theory to an unusual experiment that doomed yellow fever as one of medicine's great villains. They divided a number of soldier volunteers into two groups. The first group was placed in tents with the unwashed and stained belongings of soldiers who had died of yellow fever. The men in the second were given clean clothing and housed in sanitary quarters. But before entering, they were inoculated with the bites of the female *Aedes*.

This painting by Dean Cornwell is called "The Conquest of Yellow Fever."
It captures a dramatic moment in history. Dr. Walter Reed (standing in center)
watches as a fellow doctor is inoculated during a yellow fever experiment.

The results were all that Reed could have hoped for. The mystery behind the spread of yellow fever came to a sudden end. Not one of the volunteers living with the belongings of fever victims fell ill. But all those who had been subjected to the *Aedes* bites came down with the disease.

Brigadier General Leonard Wood, formerly the commander of the Rough Riders and now the military governor of Cuba, acted quickly on the Reed finding. As a physician himself, he knew immediately how the disease now had to be eradicated. He summoned Major William Crawford Gorgas, the army's chief sanitation officer in Cuba, and gave him a simple order: Find the female *Aedes* wherever it breeds and wipe it out.

Gorgas quickly sent troops into the streets of Havana and other areas to clear away the standing waters that were known to be the mosquito's major breeding grounds. The men cleaned street gutters, cesspools, rain barrels, puddles, and even damp spots in houses, stables, and eating places. Within three months, the work produced startling results: In Havana alone, the people were free of yellow fever for the first time since 1649. The first step had been taken in the eventual eradication of the disease.

The cleanup campaign in Havana and the voyage of a newly launched American battleship led to the next triumph fostered by the war.

In March 1898, as war clouds were gathering, the U.S.S. *Oregon* received orders to depart its San Francisco berth and join the fleet blockading Cuba. The summons sent the ship speeding down the Pacific and then around the foot of South America for a dash up the Atlantic to the Caribbean. It was a voyage of 16,000 miles (25,749 kilometers) that brought the warship to its destination in time to join Admiral Sampson's ships off Santiago for the destruction of Cervera's fleet.

The *Oregon*'s speed impressed everyone who read of the voyage. Troubling, though, was mention of those 16,000 sea miles that separated the east and west coasts of the United States. How could the navy ever protect the nation from attack with its two coasts so far apart? What was needed was a shortcut between the Atlantic and Pacific—a canal that could be cut across some narrow point in Central America.

The idea was not a new one. In the late 1700s a future president, Thomas Jefferson, had advised the U.S. government to construct such a waterway. The French, entrusting the job to engineer Ferdinand de Lesseps, had attempted to cut a path across the 50-mile (80-kilometer)-wide Isthmus of Panama in the 1880s, but had been defeated by a number of factors, among them the scourge of yellow fever. Together with malaria, it had killed more than 22,000 of the Indians, Jamaicans, Chinese, and whites who worked on the project.

Now, in the wake of the Spanish-American War, President Theodore Roosevelt arranged for the United States to attempt a cut across Panama. Before construction began, however, he sent William Crawford Gorgas to the isthmus with orders to wipe out both yellow fever and malaria (which was now known to be caused by the bite of the *Anopheles* mosquito). Major Gorgas, repeating his Cuban work, began draining away standing water wherever he found it—in lakes, ponds, streams, ditches, and puddles. Water that could not be drained was coated over with oil to kill the mosquitoes, their eggs, and larvae.

The result: By the time the digging of the Panama Canal began in 1904, yellow fever was all but gone along its route. Malaria then slowly but steadily disappeared in the following years. By 1914, the year in which the waterway was completed, both diseases posed little or no threat to the workers.

The Spanish-American War was the shortest and least damaging of American conflicts. It lasted just 114 days and, as tragic as their deaths were, claimed the lives of fewer than 500 men in battle: 469 army troops and 18 navy personnel (In addition, approximately 2,500 men died when struck down by disease). But, despite its brevity, it ranks among the most influential conflicts in American history because it completed the process of turning the United States into an international power.

Though America began the 1900s as an international power, its presence at that time was seen mainly in the Caribbean Sea and the Pacific Ocean. But in the following 100 years, the nation spread its presence—for good and for ill—to all corners of the globe. That presence was seen in World Wars I and II, in the search for international peace by the League of Nations and then the United Nations, in the country's welcome to newcomers from throughout the world, and in its astonishing technical advances that have ranged from the frightening development of nuclear weaponry to computers, to medical miracles that have saved countless lives, and on to the probes and human explorations of outer space.

Indeed, a war in all its heroism and ugliness launched what many historians have christened the American Century.

BIBLIOGRAPHY

Axelrod, Alan, and Charles Phillips. *The Macmillan Dictionary of Military Biography.* New York: Macmillan, 1998.

Brinkley, Douglas. *American Heritage History of the United States.* New York: Viking Putnam, 1998.

Carnes, Mark C., John A. Garraty, with Patrick Williams. *Mapping America's Past: A Historical Atlas.* New York: Henry Holt, 1996.

Carruth, Gorton. *The Encyclopedia of American Facts and Dates,* 9th Edition. New York: HarperCollins, 1993.

Chambers, John Whiteclay, II, ed. *The Oxford Companion to American Military History.* New York: Oxford University Press, 1999.

Cosmas, Graham A. *An Army for Empire: The United States Army in the Spanish-American War.* Columbia: University of Missouri Press, 1971.

Dierks, Jack Cameron. *A Leap to Arms.* Philadelphia: Lippincott, 1970.

Dolan, Edward F. *Walter Reed: Vanquishing Yellow Fever.* Chicago: Britannica Books, 1962.

——*Panama and the United States: Their Canal, Their Stormy Years.* New York: Franklin Watts, 1990.

Dolan, Edward F., and Margaret M. Scariano. *Cuba and the United States: Troubled Neighbors.* New York: Franklin Watts, 1987.

Evans, Harold, with Gail Buckland and Kevin Baker. *The American Century.* New York: Alfred A. Knopf, 1998.

Garraty, John A. *1,001 Things Everyone Should Know About American History.* New York: Doubleday, 1989.

Garraty, John A., and Peter Gay, editors. *The Columbia History of the World.* New York: Harper & Row, 1972.

Grenville, J. A. S. *A History of the World in the Twentieth Century.* Cambridge: Harvard University Press, 1994.

Keller, Allan. *The Spanish-American War.* New York: Hawthorn Books, 1969.

Leckie, Robert. *The Wars of America, Volume 1: From 1600 to 1900.* New York: HarperCollins, 1992.

———. *The Wars of America. Volume 2: From 1900 to 1992.* New York: HarperCollins, 1992.

Matloff, Maurice, ed. *American Military History, Volume 1: 1775-1902.* Conshohocken, PA: Combined Books, 1996.

Millett, Allan R. *Semper Fidelis: The History of the United States Marine Corps.* New York: Macmillan, 1980.

Musicant, Ivan. *Empire by Default: The Spanish-American War and the Dawn of the American Century.* New York: Henry Holt, 1998.

Nevins, Allan, and Henry Steele Commager. *A Short History of the United States,* 5th Edition. New York: Modern Library, 1966.

Perry, James M. *Arrogant Armies: Great Military Disasters and the Generals Behind Them.* New York: John Wiley & Sons, 1996.

Trask, David F. *The War with Spain in 1898.* New York: Macmillan, 1981.

Traxel, David. *1898: The Tumultuous Year of Victory, Invention, Internal Strike, and Industrial Expansion that Saw the Birth of the American Century.* New York: Alfred A. Knopf, 1998.

INDEX

Page numbers in *italics* refer to illustrations.